NEGATIVE CAPABILITY: A PHENOMENOLOGICAL STUDY OF LIVED EXPERIENCE AT THE EDGE OF CERTITUDE AND INCERTITUDE

Abstract

The study examined what it was like for leaders to be in a state of negative capability during periods of uncertainty and conflict in the workplace. "Negative Capability" is an expression that was coined by the English romantic poet John Keats and suggests a peculiar disposition to stay in mysteries, doubts, and uncertainty without the irritable reaching after fact and reason. Interviews were conducted using the interpretative phenomenological analysis (IPA) methodology. The analysis indicates that the context in which a leader is embedded does not have a significant bearing on how that individual experiences and makes sense of negative capability. The majority of leaders interviewed appear to have a diminished capacity to contain uncertainty when faced with paradoxical dilemmas. In these situations, they resort to behaviors such as problem solving, consulting others, shutting down, and dispersing as a means of defending against the uncertainty. Exercising servant leadership and the intermingling of the leaders' personal and professional lives are strongly emerging themes.

Keywords: John Keats, negative capability, OCD, paradox, levels of abstraction, certitude, dialectics, Buddhism, dispersal, social defenses, reframing.

UMI 3624967

ProQuest LLC.
789 East Eisenhower Parkway
P.O. Box 1346
Ann Arbor, MI 48106 - 1346

Dedication

As I provide final closure to this 11-year journey and explore what lies ahead, I dedicate this work with great fondness to my wife Marilyn, who almost singlehandedly held the fort for many years and enabled me to realize my academic dream. Without her love, confidence, and support, this would not have been possible. I am also very grateful to my daughters Ratna and Preeya who unconditionally believed in me even when things became rough. They have been my sounding boards, technology gurus, and creative artists.

My life's work would feel incomplete without a dedication to my late mother-in-law Christine Pinto who never lost faith in me even when I questioned my own self-worth. Mummy, you will live in my heart forever. This one's for you! Finally, my deepest gratitude to my parents Sanat and Usha Behal who have been waiting with bated breath and cheering me on as I approach the finish line.

Acknowledgements

I gratefully acknowledge many academics that have touched my life very meaningfully since I joined the Fielding Graduate University as a doctoral student. First and foremost, my mentor, friend, and chair Bob Silverman, PhD without whose encouragement and inspiration I would probably not see this day. My heartfelt thanks also go to the faculty readers Steve Schapiro, EdD and Annabelle Nelson, PhD who made an enormous contribution over the years to my growth and transformation as a scholar. To Sharon Davis Brown, student reader, a big thanks for your support. And finally, thanks to Amy L. Fraher, EdD, external examiner who provided valuable input from the standpoint of organizational psychodynamics.

There are many other individuals that have supported me in this exciting journey. I am unable to mention everyone by name; however please know how much I have appreciated your camaraderie over the years. I would like to extend a special word of thanks to the 14 leaders who gave so generously of their time and shared their lived experiences with great candor. I also owe a debt of gratitude to the following Fielding colleagues who selflessly reached out to me with their wisdom, insight, and suggestions as I struggled to navigate difficult terrain over the past few years: Michael Joseph Serabian, PhD, Steve Wallis, PhD, Susan Quash-Mah, PhD, and Michele Vincenti, PhD. Finally, a word of thanks to Valerie Malhotra Bentz, PhD and David Allan Rehorick, PhD for sharing with me their work on transformative phenomenology.

Table of Contents

LIST OF APPENDICES

BOXES AND FIGURES

Chapter One

Preface

The danger (of this enterprise), in short is that instead of providing a basis for what already exists, one is forced to advance beyond familiar territory, far from the certainties to which one is accustomed, towards an as yet uncharted land and unforeseeable conclusion. (Foucault, 1972, p. 39)

I initially came across the Keatsian expression "negative capability" in a paper by French (2000) in which the author makes important linkages between the poet's aesthetic notion, dispersal, and the containment of emotion. I was so captivated by the phenomenon that I continue to follow with great curiosity, the work of French and his colleagues at the University of the West of England. While the authors provide a good foundation of the construct from a leadership standpoint, I also realize that in order to better understand the complexity of something, one must first come to terms with one's own ignorance.

Cusa (1440) suggests that, as we accumulate knowledge, the darkness of "unlearned ignorance" is diminished; however, the more knowledge we acquire and the more we learn, the greater our awareness of how much we still do not know. This new awareness, he refers to as "learned ignorance." I make an analogy between the notion of "unlearned ignorance" and Bion's (1984a) formulation of "knowing" which he described using the symbol "K." In direct contrast to the former, Bion conceptualized "O" as the ultimate embodiment of truth that is unknown and unknowable. While this truth-in-the-moment may never enter the realm of knowledge and certitude, he believed that it is through the encounter at the edge of knowing and not knowing that we may come under its influence. As Eigen (1998) writes, "It can be creatively explosive, traumatically wounding, crushingly uplifting" (Eigen, 1998, p. 78). As I make sense of my own uncertainty, it seems as though I am lost in reverie,[1] allowing myself to be receptive and yet, perturbed by the experience.

Introduction

"Negative Capability" is not an expression that is very familiar outside the realm of English literature. Even those who have read Keats may not be particularly conversant with the construct—after all, the poet only used it once in a letter to his brothers in a moment of intense speculation. It is a unique capacity for introspection when we are open to thoughts, feelings, and sensation, such that we are able to stay with mysteries, doubts, uncertainties, and ambiguity without the irritable reaching after fact and reason (Keats, 1817). Anyone who has been in a transient paradoxical state of mind is perhaps familiar with the tension of staying at the edge of knowing and not knowing, as the mind attempts to seize something concrete to hold onto.

As leaders, we are often called upon to address and solve complex organizational issues; however, we sometimes look for solutions based on our past experiences or future assumptions. We are conditioned to learn from mistakes and plan for the future in order to avoid making the same mistakes again. The reality of the present is often overlooked.

Simpson and French (2006) posit that attending to the present is a refrain, both ancient and modern, steeped in Eastern and Western philosophy. It implies the ability to live with uncertainty, tolerate frustration, and make room for multiple perspectives that may require a certain degree of patience and passive acceptance. The authors suggest that the practice of negative capability calls upon us to remain in this unsettling mental space in order to face the terrifying pressure of the present where most problems seem to reside. The refrain that they address, is refraining from action. "In the pressure of the moment, 'what we know' may not be available to us. What we thought we know, or did indeed knew once, can disappear in action when we are 'under fire,' to use Bion's metaphor" (Simpson and French, 2006, p. 245). As a paradoxical state of mind it seems ephemeral at best, and yet, without understanding and negotiating this paradox, it would be difficult to perform a task, which by its very nature, demands this unique skill. Does acknowledging our own ignorance enable us to be open to the ever-present dynamics and perplexity of the present? I expound on this in the next chapter.

An idea so rich—steeped in the dialectic of predictability and unpredictability, captivates my imagination and inspires me to understand it better, for I see parallels between the poetic notion and my work with leaders. The predictability comes from the fact that all leaders from time to time are thrust into conditions of uncertainty and perplexity. Ironically though, holding this tension requires a unique state of mind---a peculiar disposition such as "negative capability" where one is comfortable with doubt, uncertainty, and unpredictability. Batchelor (1990) suggests that "such doubt is neither a cognitive hinge, nor a psychological defect, but a state of existential perplexity" (Batchelor, 1990, p. 16).

Many occupations today demand that leaders have a certain degree of comfort with doubt and uncertainty and can stay in that perturbed mental space in order to do their jobs. Some examples are academia, organizational development, psychotherapy, consulting, and conflict mediation. I illustrate the use of this skill by means of a case study from my own practice.

Case scenario

One of my coaching clients who is Vice President (HR) of a sales organization recently approached me to work with her company's senior leadership team that includes the chief executive officer (CEO), chief operating officer (COO), and 10 regional directors, each heading a departmental unit. During my initial consultation with the CEO, he lamented, "The team is not functioning like a well-oiled machine." He had started to notice serious breakdown in communication and increasing rivalry and conflict among certain directors. He commented that he had tried everything to resolve the situation and was now ready to make some drastic changes unless he could see a way through (I refer here to the CEO's positive capabilities, that is what he knows about the situation based on his past experience). His body language and demeanor suggested a state of helplessness and frustration, as he struggled to make sense of the situation.

As I listened to the CEO's account, I found myself rather perturbed, particularly by his comment about the team not functioning like a "well-oiled machine," a metaphor that came as a surprise to me. As we talked, he made another comment in which he implicated one of his directors as the "problem child" who was causing the conflict among the team members. I was worried about the possibility that he might be scapegoating the director, and in the process, absolving himself and the rest of his team from any wrongdoing.

As we met again, I broached the topic of not knowing, that is, what was it that he and I were not addressing and taking ownership of in the current situation? He seemed perplexed at first; even a bit irritated, as though I was questioning his judgment and competence. I persisted because I wanted us both to come to terms with how eagerly we were focusing on the manifest (the known variable), while ignoring the empty spaces around it (the unknown). There was a long pause as I sat in complete silence and started to get in touch with my own ignorance and lack of knowledge about what might be happening in the situation. To my amazement, the CEO shortly began to mirror my silence without interrupting it, and we both sat there, quietly reflecting.

He finally spoke and admitted that he might himself be getting in the way of his own team's progress and that it was unfair of him to target one of the directors, referring to him as the "problem child." This was a new awareness that he had not previously come to terms with. So, in a sense, by creating the negative space between us and holding the tensionality without succumbing to polarization, we may have made room for new thoughts. Using Bollas (1987) conceptualization of the "unthought known," something new was born that may have been previously out of conscious awareness. Following Keats, the CEO and I allowed our minds to become "a thoroughfare for whatever it is that would surface." We chose to remain in doubt and mystery without the irritable reaching after fact and reason, which may have been jeopardized, had the CEO dispersed into a string of rationalization or explanation.

Leaders often find themselves in difficult situations such as this, when the pressure to react is strong. Israelstam (2007) suggests that tensions evoked in dialectically charged situations often create new spaces for learning and growth that are related to mindless states. I suggest that negative capability may be a transient phase--- an ephemeral state of mind that is difficult to hold indefinitely. The impulse to act may be contained (resisted) through reflective inaction or dispersed (realized) through action. Both scenarios may progress to a new, more enduring state—the opposition between two interacting forces, both of which may appear to be contradictory or complementary.

4

Regardless of whether a leader exercises refrain or decides to take quick action, these tensions may never be truly resolved.

Research question

What is it like for leaders to be in a state of negative capability during periods of uncertainty and conflict in the workplace?

I suggest that negative capability represents a dialectical tension that is virtually endemic to the human condition. We are thrust into these perplexing spaces wittingly and unwittingly. These discursive tensions are evoked in every relationship, regardless of whether it is personal or professional and may be defined as core tensions or opposing values that arise when two seemingly incompatible forces coexist in the mind. Some examples might be the dichotomous relationship between autonomy and connectedness, disclosure and secrecy, and intimacy and abstraction. We seem to oscillate between these values, often unconsciously, and may view them as contradictions or internal conflicts. These conflicts may sometimes produce the opposite of what we are trying to accomplish. By directing the research question to leaders in different contexts, I hoped that I might be able to understand better how these tensions are evoked, managed, and negotiated.

Baxter and Montgomery (1996), discussing the "relational dialectics theory," posit that these tensions are ongoing and develop over time. They are the discursive lubricant that allows meaning to emerge between discourses. I discuss their work in more detail in the literature review, under the section entitled "dialogism and dialectics." When organizations undergo periods of rapid change and uncertainty, it seems that a leader's capacity to hold the negative space seriously diminishes, while patience and reflection give way to dispersal.

When we are faced by the emotional impact of not knowing and cannot come to terms with our own vulnerability, our tendency is to avoid that painful experience. Needleman (1990) posits that to meet "the question" (not knowing) must inevitably mean facing the terrifying pressure of our own ignorance. It suggests staying in an inquiring mode and being content with the perturbations of the moment. The author uses the term "dispersal" to denote the patterns of avoidance that we engage in unconsciously in order to contain our anxiety.

French (2000) suggests three forms of dispersal: dispersal into activity, dispersal into emotional reactions, and dispersal into explanations. He writes, "In individuals and in groups, habits of dispersal become established with great rapidity: the higher the anxiety level, the quicker this can happen. In organizational contexts, on the other hand, patterns of dispersal tend to evolve more gradually" (French, 2000, p. 6). These patterns of dispersal may over time become so engrained in the organizational culture, that in order to do one's job, one may have to hold in the mind, what appear to be two dialectically opposed, even contradictory positions. These ongoing tensions may result in the formation of "social defenses" (Jacques, 1955; Menzies, 1960; Czander; 1993). An example of this tension may be a leader's inability to stay calm and think, when the pressure to react may be very strong. In succumbing to this pressure, the individual over time loses the capacity to reflect, and instead unconsciously engages in defensive routines. This may take the form of overcompensation, exaggerated responses, and ritualistic behavior such as checking and rechecking things.

In perplexing situations, leaders can consciously deploy negative capability when the pressure to react seems to take precedence over patience and thoughtful reflection. The problem, however is that for many leaders, this skill remains underdeveloped. They are recruited because they possess other positive capabilities such as technical functional skills and business acumen, but not the attributes that are essential from the standpoint of practicing negative capability. I discuss these important attributes below in the context of a leadership assessment instrument. It could be an important instrument that identifies how a leader's direct reports and peers perceive that individual's capacity for negative capability. When used in conjunction with appropriate interventions and training, there is a possibility that organizations may develop a future cadre of leaders that are more aware and adept at deploying nontraditional skills such as negative capability.

Negative Capability 360-Feeback Model

In 2009, I partnered with a company in New York City that custom designs leadership assessment tools. We jointly produced a new 360 Degree prototype that measures leaders' competencies in several key areas germane to negative capability. Roca (2009) published a press release that announced the launch. At that time, the

6

initiative was an early effort based on what we believed to be leadership attributes that were important from the standpoint of negative capability. The prototype was supported by our observations and experience, but not direct empirical data. We experimented with the model in an online leadership course on negative capability where participants' peers and direct reports were asked to assess their leaders' competencies in 8 key areas. This study was an attempt to understand how leaders make sense of negative capability, and also explore avenues for its future application, such as the development of this model into a viable instrument. Figure 1.1 below is a schematic representation of the "NC 360 Feedback Model."

Figure 1.1 (Schematic representation of the NC 360 Feedback Model)

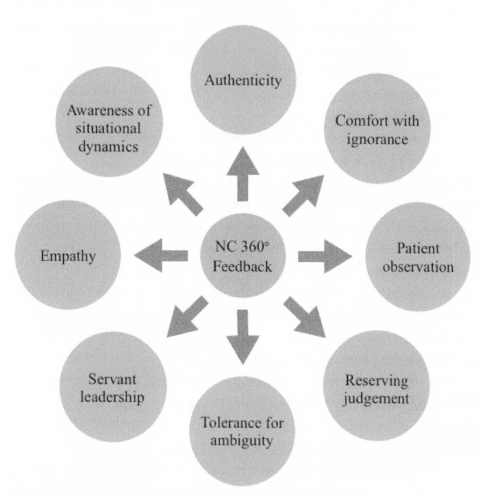

The 8 leadership competencies that were identified are outlined below:

1. Authenticity: Measures transparency in actions and purpose so that others understand our motives and know what to expect from the leader.

2. Comfort with ignorance: Confronting, accepting, and sharing the bounds of one's personal knowledge in order to gain the benefit of the group's knowledge.

3. Patient observation: Delays immediate action and observes results of employed strategies in order to get more information before taking further action.

4. Reserving judgment: Holding off on making decisions and remaining open to various possible outcomes until more information is available, so that the leader makes use of what others know, gathers relevant data, and makes informed choices.

5. Tolerance for ambiguity: Maintaining objectivity, clarity of purpose, and a level head amidst uncertainty in order to sustain good decision making ability and engender confidence in those around the leader.

6. Servant leadership: Be comfortable with vulnerability, put others' interests before our own, and become a true servant of those that we lead.

7. Empathy: Being sensitive to others' emotions in order to help them feel understood, free up their creative energy for productive use, and provide for their emotional needs.

8. Awareness of situational dynamics: Being aware of the situation and the role one plays in it, so that there is a better understanding of how the leader may have contributed to the dynamic.

The literature cited in the study informs each of these areas. Batchelor (1990), Bion (1984a), and Eigen (1998) address "comfort with ignorance" and "tolerance for ambiguity." Greenleaf (2008) discusses "empathy" and "authenticity" in the context of "servant leadership." Batchelor (1990, 2000) elucidates "patient observation" and "reserving judgment." Bolman & Deal (2008) and Elson (2010) discuss "awareness of situational dynamics." It is beyond the scope of this chapter to engage in a comprehensive discussion of these attributes; however I consider them to be important enough from the standpoint of negative capability. Chapter 5 contains a more thorough discussion of some of these attributes as they relate to the phenomenon.

Chapter two provides a literature review of interrelated theories and paradigmatic frameworks that inform the study. These include conversations from the field of organizational psychodynamics and the work of contemporary theorists who have extrapolated the concept of negative capability to developing a better understanding of leadership and leader behavior. The work of classical theorists as it relates to attention and interpretation is outlined. Additionally, literature from poetry, Tibetan and Zen Buddhism, and dialogism and dialectics is reviewed in order to explore the connections between these meta-theoretical perspectives and the topic of the study. In addition to these core conversations, I also discuss paradoxical thinking and entanglements. Finally, I make reference to communicative space in action science where the practice of negative capability finds application.

Chapter three delineates a qualitative research methodology entitled "Interpretative Phenomenological Analysis" (IPA), which was deployed to study negative capability. It begins with a discussion of the theoretical foundations of IPA, illuminated by means of two separate studies conducted by scholars who deployed the methodology. The study design is presented, based on the findings of the pilot study. Other items such as the recruitment and selection of study participants, data collection and management, general assumptions, and areas of research are also discussed. IPA expects that the bracketed assumptions of the researcher be disclosed in order to share with the reader what might have been the limitations and challenges of conducting such research. These have been summarized.

Chapter four deals with data analysis and interpretation. It contains 14 individual cases, accompanied by interpretations from the researcher. Selected extracts from the interview transcripts are produced in order to introduce the reader to the participants' life worlds. An initial listing of emergent themes appears at the end of the study, following the appendices. A clustering of emergent themes and a combined master listing of superordinate themes are also shown. Finally, I provide a group-level narrative, including a schematic representation of holding polarities and paradox.

The final chapter contains a meta-theoretical exploration of uncertainty and negative capability, findings, and experience of conducting the study. A postmodern definition of negative capability is also offered.

The phenomenological study was an attempt to understand the lived experience of leaders who had experienced the phenomenon of negative capability during periods of uncertainty and conflict in the workplace. It is important to emphasize that given the highly abstract nature and obscurity of negative capability, the study was designed so as to research the phenomenon sideways and not directly. Exploring a phenomenon "sideways" means understanding aspects that are not readily available to the researcher as direct lived experience, but instead manifest by immersing in a participant's life world. Therefore, the study explored how leaders made sense of uncertainty, paradox, and conflict, which are conditions that are associated with the negative capability frame of mind. In order to understand the essence of the phenomenon, it was important to explore those conditions.

CHAPTER TWO

Literature review

Dewey (1929a) examines how scholars and philosophers use preset concepts and methods as a quest for certainty in order to shield themselves from the emotional storm. Star (2007), referring to the work of Dewey, suggests "that this quest for certainty (for example, a single model that pre-explains most events in the world) is a way of shielding ourselves from the powerful pain of attachment-separation grief" (Star, 2007, p. 87). It is in the paradoxical holding together of attachment and separation that we truly experience what it means to be alive--to be both abstract and intimate. It is not that we strive as adults for total abstraction (separation) or total intimacy (attachment). Indeed, Winnicott argues that an important part of maturation involves striking a balance between managing the anxiety of separation with the need for attachment (Winnicott, 1965). But it is in our very struggle to achieve a balance between separation and relatedness, that we also experience a great deal of turbulence and uncertainty. We seem to alleviate our anxiety by taking a polarized (either-or stance), or as Winnicott suggests, through the use of transitional objects we contain a bit of both worlds, without being either one in totality.

We can think of this ambiguous mental state as being in a liminal space, standing at the threshold of a boundary and on both ends, but not fully present on either side (van Gennep, 1960; Turner, 1994). Liminality now includes structural changes in society where established orders once taken for granted, are being questioned and put into doubt and uncertainty. This presents new challenges for leaders who may have been accustomed to a style that does not make room for paradoxical thinking (Johnson, 1992).

There are several theoretical frameworks that inform "negative capability." I am presenting here key fields of inquiry that illuminate the phenomenon directly or indirectly.

Organizational Psychodynamics

I turn to the work of scholars in the field of organizational psychodynamics that have borrowed Keats's construct in order to better understand group dynamics and leader behavior. It is hoped that exploring negative capability from the standpoint of leadership, may enrich our understanding of how leaders make sense of the phenomenon.

French (2002) extrapolates the concept to his work in organizational consulting. While the paper has a psychoanalytic focus, the ideas posited by the author set the stage for future work in the field. He writes, "Effective work in the field addressed by ISPSO (International Society for the Psychoanalytic Study of Organizations) demands of us a particular kind of attention. This state of mind depends on our 'Negative Capability,' that is, on our capacity for thinking and feeling, for learning and containment, for abstention and indifference" (French, 2002, p.1). "Thus, 'Negative Capability' describes the capacity to experience emotion, one's own and others,' but also to contain it for the sake of the work, and by doing so, to learn from and to use emotion to inform our understanding of the work" (French, 1999: 1218).

French et al endorse the notion that negative space does not imply the lack of something or a deficiency. On the contrary, it reflects the human capacity to create expansiveness, while resisting the pressure to react. It calls upon us to be comfortable with our own ignorance. It means leaving open the space for new thoughts and ideas to emerge; thoughts that do not yet have a thinker (Simpson & French, 2006).

In his work on attention and observation, Bion (1970) writes, "Any session should be judged by comparison with the Keats formulation so as to guard against one commonly unobserved fault leading to analysis 'interminable.' The fault lies in the failure to observe and is intensified by the inability to appreciate the significance of observation" (Bion, 1970, p.125). Leaders carry out a lot of work in groups these days, and it is important to understand the dynamics, especially those undercurrents which are not readily manifest, but play a significant role in shaping the life of a group. Bion

13

(1961) developed the construct of the "basic assumptions group" as an unconscious flight from the "work group." When confronted with a task, a faction of the group that is unable to contain the uncertainty inherent in the task itself, unconsciously disperses into one of three "basic assumptions," namely BaD (basic assumptions dependency), BaP (basic assumptions pairing), and BaF/F (basic assumptions fight/flight).

Members of a group often oscillate between process and content; between togetherness and separateness; between intimacy and abstraction, as a means of not confronting the task, fighting the leader, pairing with other members, or fleeing from the group (mentally or physically)---anything that will distract or derail them from the task. The desire to sabotage the work is unconscious for the most part and may stem from the inability to hold the paradox represented by the dialectics between the "Work Group" and the "Basic Assumptions Group."

Nitsun (1996) describes a conceptual framework within which to explore the dialectical tension in an analytical group. Any phenomenon, by its very nature, gives rise to its opposite: good and evil, night and day, cold and hot. These polarities are interrelated and depend on each other for their existence. The dialectical interplay between these poles unites the opposites, such that they can be held together. Morgan (1986) also addresses this phenomenon as occurring in the life of a group. He encourages us to embrace the naturally occurring forces of contradiction and flux and suggests that control always generates counter control; organization may lead to disorganization, and success to a potential downfall.

Ogden (1992a) sees the dialectic as a process in which contradictory elements both create and negate each other and neither of the elements has any phenomenological meaning without a relationship to the other. In this study, I suggest that negative capability may not exist without this dialectical interplay. The very notion of "staying in mysteries, doubts, and uncertainty without the irritable reaching after fact and reason" (Keats, 1817) represents a tension.

French writes that when we are confronted with a question that impacts us emotionally, we are faced with one of two choices—either contain the impulses and anxiety while being content with half-knowledge, or disperse (French, 2000). Dispersal, as used in this context means to flee into action, explanation, rationalization and a host

14

of other reactions that may be defenses against the anxiety of not knowing. While the act of dispersal may temporarily alleviate the anxiety, our inability to contain the impulse, perpetuates it and may set in motion an unconscious ritual. It is not that the person who is capable of sitting with the anxiety is any less anxious; however, through the exercise of refrain and choosing to remain in a state of doubt, we may be better able to hold the paradox and make room for new thoughts and feelings to emerge in the negative space.

While on this topic, it is important to make a note of the systemic nature of dispersal in contemporary organizations. In general, the higher the anxiety levels, the more diminished the capacity to contain, and consequently, the greater our need to disperse. Be it on an individual, group, or organizational level, once dispersal becomes habitual, spaces may no longer be available for thinking and reflection. Over time, this tendency may contribute to the formation of defensive routines (also known as social defenses). Action may become an escape, even an unconscious attack as a defense against the anxiety of facing the present reality.

Argyris (1990) suggests that when we are free to act as we wish, but do so in ways that are counterproductive to the organization, we are engaging in defensive reasoning. We realize that certain actions are questionable, but we choose to not address them. He cites several causes for defensive reasoning such as a leader's tendency to want to be in control, especially when facing the threat of embarrassment. "Theories-in-use are the master programs that individuals hold in order to be in control. Model I theory-in-use instructs individuals to seek to be in unilateral control, to win, and not to upset people" (p. 13). Most scholars would agree that sitting with and reflecting on the uncertainty and doubt may be more difficult than dealing with it in the moment.

An understanding of systems psychodynamics[2] as a perspective (lens) in organizational development (OD) work is important for investigating much of what happens unconsciously in groups. The dialectics of development contain both, a compulsive push toward growth and an equally strong regressive pull toward task evasion. This dynamic tension is not completely resolved; however, Bion believed that the work group triumphs in the end. Fraher (2004) writes about these tensions in her essay on group relations theory.[3]

French et al (2001) propose a new way of conceptualizing great leadership qualities by thinking and reflecting on them in terms of negative capability. They suggest that leaders who have the capacity to resist dispersing into knowing and action when faced with organizational pressures and anxiety are better able to create space for themselves and others at the edge of certainty and uncertainty. It is at the edge between certainty and uncertainty that successful leaders form a capacity for creative thought by embracing both negative and positive capabilities (French, Harvey & Simpson, 2001). Ward (1963) writes: "Negative Capability suggests a peculiarly human capacity to live with and tolerate ambiguity and paradox, and to remain content with half knowledge" (Ward, 1963, p. 161). It indicates a non-defensive way of dealing with change, a capacity to contain patiently, flexibility of character, and most of all, a willingness to dissolve the ego and tolerate a loss of self. Through recreating oneself in another, the leader becomes like the strings of a lyre, not to create music, but to remain open to organizational inquiry (Scott, 1969).

This is further explicated in the work of other theorists. Reason (1994), for example, suggests that transformational leadership "is based on an effort to be aware of the present moment in all its fullness, recognizing that such effort can never be completely successful. "Transforming power is not just open to feedback, but is actively vulnerable in seeking challenge and contradiction, seeking out ways in which its exercise is blind and unaware" (Reason, 1994, pp. 331-32). The Zen Buddhism refrain of staying in the present moment and allowing all thoughts and feelings to come and go unencumbered is deeply reflected in Bion's advice to his analyst to "impose on himself a positive discipline of eschewing memory and desire" (Bion, 1970, p. 31). By remaining in the present without engaging in past memories and desires, the analyst is more able to contain the ever-present need to disperse.

As I begin to think about the paradoxical nature of negative capability, I am reminded of my own work in the area of transformative learning and adult education. Learning breakthroughs occur at the edge of knowing and not knowing--a liminal state where you often stand at the edge and on both ends of the boundary. Many adult learners find themselves in this anxiety-producing transient state of mind. How they negotiate this space may determine what they take away from the experience. Earlier in

16

this paper I have discussed how such spaces are not readily available in organizations. Laiken writes:

> It has been said, "the unexamined life is not worth living." Yet, in the current work and educational climate of increasing pressure to produce relentlessly, the most important factor for success has been all but eliminated. This is the ability to create a space for collective reflection, learning, and ultimately personal, organizational, and potentially social, transformation. Our recent research (Laiken, 2001; Laiken, Edge, Friedman & West, forthcoming) has highlighted managing the paradox of task versus process, or action versus reflection, as a critical factor in blocking or conversely, facilitating, transformative learning. (Laiken, 2002, p. 3)

These paradoxes are never resolved. They are like the pendulum that oscillates between two polarities, but is not at either polarity for an extended period of time. Like negative capability, this too represents a dialectical tension, an oscillation between action and reflection. Laiken writes that the opportunity to reflect on our lived experience is a critical piece of transformation and may result in profound behavioral and attitudinal changes (Lewin, 1951; Argyris and Schon, 1978; Kolb, 1984; Mezirow, 1991; Cranton, 1994). Partly in keeping with the notion of transformation, this study is an investigation of the lived experience of participants who are making sense of the dialectics of certainty and uncertainty.

Organizations that make space for critical thinking and reflection may experience increased production capacity and improved employee morale. It demands having the wisdom and patience to slow down in order to later speed up (Cranton, 1994). "Critical reflection in organizations seems to be relegated to an isolated corner, if it is supported at all. People are so consumed with doing vs. being that they do not put in the time to build teamwork" (Laiken, 2002, p. 5).

The comments from Laiken and Cranton remind me of my own growth and transformation over the years and the work that I have done with colleagues in small group settings. It is in the struggle between autonomy and togetherness that we seem to experience transformational learning breakthroughs. While vacillation may seem contradictory and indecisive, one way of holding a paradox is to remain content with

17

half-knowledge without succumbing to the ever-present pressure to react, resolve, and find quick answers to life's perplexing questions. Adult learners that I have worked with in group relations conference settings in the Tavistock tradition, report profound changes when their anxiety is greatly heightened, they are thrust into doubt, and are called upon to contain that anxiety as opposed to acting it out. The ability to slow down, reflect, refrain, and wait in patience, seems to run contrary to the current organizational notion of speed, efficacy, answers, and clarity, all of which seem to take a higher status. Unfortunately, patience is not seen as virtue, but often equated with being lackadaisical and lazy.

Raab (1997) discusses the "terrible anxiety experienced by both clients and consultant (students and lecturer) when forced to stay in the present and face their own unknowingness. Traditional models of learning operate without acknowledging the extent of this anxiety and offer little insight into the ways in which teachers unconsciously collude with their students in their attempt to escape from it" (Raab, 1997, p. 161). The author suggests that reframing the teacher's traditional role as consultant is one way of working with that anxiety and harnessing it productively. It entails cultivating an expertise in not knowing, of staying with the questions and helping students remain in that space, rather than seeking knowledge in order to fill it. By contrast, taking the traditional role of expert in knowing often means mobilizing structure and control as two defenses against the anxiety of not knowing. The role of not knowing demands that a teacher be vulnerable enough to access her own ignorance and remain open to surprise and emergence. Paradoxically, vulnerability may be an unusual quandary. It invokes a great deal of fear and anxiety on the one hand, but may also have a liberating effect on the other.

Bion (1961) discusses how the hatred of learning through experience unleashes a great deal of terror because people come face-to-face with their not knowing. So, it is clearly incumbent upon a leader or an educator to provide a safe container for the group's anxiety while resisting the temptation to be immobilized by it. It is this dialectic which is at the heart of most group work of an experiential nature. What is manifest (conscious) in the group is perhaps as important as that which is tacit (unconscious). The importance of unconscious dynamics in learning groups cannot be underestimated.

18

As an example, one of the reasons why teachers and consultants find themselves in the role of experts in knowing is because their students project knowledge and expertise onto them. In raising the experts to a pedestal, the learners or clients may assume a dependency role that feels safe.

Mezirow et al (2000) have offered critical perspectives in transformative learning and adult education. Schein (1999) discussing the critical importance of accessing one's ignorance writes: "The only way I can discover my own inner reality is to distinguish what I know from what I assume to know, from what I truly do not know. I cannot determine what is the current reality if I do not get in touch with what I do not know about the situation and do not have the wisdom to ask about it" (Schein, 1999, p. 11).

I have made previous references to liminality in this study because I see a parallel with dialectics. Meyer and Land (2006) suggest, "learning involves the occupation of a liminal space during the process of the mastery of a threshold concept. This space is likened to that which adolescents inhabit; not yet adults, not quite children (sic). It is an 'unstable space' in which the learner may oscillate between old and emergent understandings" (Meyer & Land, 2006, p. 22). I see liminality as a point of departure, a temporary/transitional space, much like "negative capability" where one may stand at or on both sides of a boundary or threshold. Turner (1969) discusses liminality as the midpoint in a status-sequence between two positions, 'outsiderhood' which refers to actions and relationships, which do not flow from a recognized social status, while 'lowermost' status refers to the lowest rung in a system.

Winnicott (1960), a British object relations theorist first conceptualized the idea of a holding environment created by the mother for the purpose of holding and containing an infant's anxieties. The mother accomplishes this through love, empathy, understanding, and dependable patience. Once the holding environment has been created, a mediating transitional space (such as the one in negative capability) may emerge, which facilitates pretend play, exploration, and experimentation that are all important for growth and creativity. Bion (1967) also developed the concepts of the "container" and "contained," which he used extensively in therapy and group work. He believed that the mother acts as the "container" for the infant's raw and unmetabolized anxieties, detoxifies (transforms) them, and returns them to the child in a form that is

19

more soothing and easy digestible. I now discuss another meta-theoretical framework that informs negative capability.

Tibetan and Zen Buddhism

Batchelor is a noted proponent of agnostic or secular Buddhism. A renowned author and a former Tibetan and Zen Buddhist monk by training, he is considered to be one of the foremost scholars on Nagarjuna and the Buddhist doctrine of the "middle way." Born into a Western world no longer immersed in the certitude of faith and belief, Batchelor fled its anxieties to embrace his new calling in Tibetan Buddhist orthodoxy. That too did not provide him the truth and solace that he was seeking, and once again he found himself drowned in doubt and uncertainty. This time, however, he began to view the uncertainty not as despair, but creative possibility. After fleeing from the dogmatism of Tibetan Buddhism , he soon began training in Zen which values questions over answers and uncertainty and perplexity over belief and certitude. To him, it was indeed, a new way forward.

"Where there is great questioning, there is great awakening. Where there is little questioning, there is little awakening. Where there is no questioning, there is no awakening" says Batchelor (1990; 2000). He describes Nagarjuna as a liminal figure (ca: 150-250 CE) who neither fits into the era of early Buddhism, nor in the late Mahayana tradition. In abandoning the need for dualism, and suspending the power of comparison, we may indeed embrace the middle way, says Batchelor. In this quest for the sublime, we paradoxically experience the dialectics of great awe and great terror. Batchelor thinks of negative capability as similar in nature to the meditative stance of Zen Buddhism where the monk or practitioner is able to focus attention on the questions, as opposed to seeking answers. It is this staying with uncertainty and not rushing into explanations, which he finds analogous to the Keatsian notion.

The Buddhist tenet of no mind[4] is an example of how the creation of negative space in meditation makes room for something new and yet un-thought to emerge. In order to know something, we have to let go of the need for knowing and instead embrace the notion of not knowing. It is through resisting action that we can truly understand the concept of reflective inaction. The moment we act, we are fleeing from the state of passive reflection. We are no longer in that negative space of disinterestedness, meaning that we are filling it with what we know and can get done. I think of negative capability as a state of being as opposed to a state of doing---of paradoxically embracing negative and positive capabilities while resisting the temptation to polarize and hold one polarity at the expense of the other. The skill lies in the capacity to move between the two positions.

Suzuki (1949) discussing the dialectics of no-mind writes, "As the attainment of Tao does not involve a continuous movement from error to truth, from ignorance to enlightenment, from mayoi[5] to satori[6], the Zen masters all proclaim that there is no enlightenment whatsoever which you can claim to have attained. Not to have is to have; silence is thunder; ignorance is enlightenment" (p-27). These paradoxical truths are known as koans[7] in Zen and are believed to invoke abrupt changes in the student.

Suler (1993) suggests that a "paradox is a statement or behavior that is seemingly inconsistent, absurd, or self-contradictory, yet in fact true. Paradoxical injunctions such as 'Disobey me!' turns disobeying into obeying and obeying into disobeying when the command turns back and enlists itself as an example of its own directive" (p-321). A double bind[8] therefore occurs when a self-contradictory statement turns back and reflects on itself, calling into question the very truth that it negates

Dialogism and dialectics

In addition to organizational psychodynamics and Buddhism, dialogism and dialectics are meta-theoretical paradigms that are core conversations, which inform the study. They address the sophisticated subtleties of negative capability in a way that none of the other paradigms can achieve singularly. While the literature on dialectics does make occasional references to Keats's aesthetic concept, no studies were found that directly address the phenomenon from the standpoint of dialectics[9].

The origin of dialogism as a philosophical doctrine is attributed to the Russian philosopher Bakhtin (1984), who until recently was best known in literary circles only. It would be fair to say that "dialogism" has not been a part of mainstream social science, and scholars interested in studying interpersonal relationships are only just beginning to reference his work. "Dialectics" has its roots in "dialogism," therefore it may be important to understand its meaning and significance. Bakhtin believed dialogue to be the essence of all interpersonal communication. Unlike monologue, dialogue is multivocal and characterized by at least two distinct voices.

Bakhtin (1981) writes, "our own discourse is gradually and slowly wrought out of others' words that have been acknowledged and assimilated" (Bakhtin, 1981, p. 345). He comments about and contrasts dialogic and monologic works. Unlike the latter, Bakhtin believed that dialogic work informs and is informed by previous works. It is an ongoing, bidirectional conversation between language and discourse (both past and present). Bakhtin (1984) further suggests that all meaning making is a dialogue and may be understood literally and metaphorically as a fusion of different systems and discourses. Participants engaged in dialogue must to some extent fuse their perspectives in order to construct a shared meaning. Conversation then is a form of unity of different perspectives, even though participants retain their own unique perspectives on the topic. Multiple perspectives on the same phenomenon, co-constructed by the participants and myself added a richness and depth to the study.

Dialogism has been around for thousands of years in ancient cultures such as China, India, and Japan. It has helped shape these cultures very dramatically, and yet it seems difficult to provide a singular answer or definition of what constitutes dialogism. More contemporary authors such as Altman, Vinsel, and Brown (1981) look at dialogism as having two meanings: (1) a style of reasoning used to establish the truth and validity of ideas, and (2) a worldview or conception of the nature of phenomena. Both are germane to this study, particularly given its phenomenological focus and methodology. It is important here to make a distinction between a dialogic process (Bakhtin, 1984) and a dialectic process (Hegel, 1977; 2003), despite the complementarity of the two constructs:

-Various existential approaches seem to coexist in a dialogic process. It does not have a great deal of rigidity and strategies are open to changes. The outcome is often open-ended and no closure is typically sought.

-In a dialectical process as conceptualized and formulated by Hegel, the goal seems to be to merge point and counterpoint (thesis and antithesis), thereby arriving at a compromise (synthesis). The end result of the process is a desired outcome---a solution that establishes primacy over other alternatives.

In constructing their grand theory of "relational dialectics," Baxter and

Montgomery (1996) choose to use the words dialogism and dialectics interchangeably, even though Bakhtin and other scholars have made a distinction between the two seemingly alike, but different constructs. They write: "To Bakhtin (1984), the essence of dialogue is its simultaneous differentiation from, yet fusion with another. To enact dialogue, the parties need to fuse their perspectives while maintaining the uniqueness of their individual perspectives" (p. 24). "Just as dialogue is simultaneously unity and difference, Bakhtin (1981) regarded all social processes as the product of 'a contradiction-ridden, tension-filled unity of two embattled tendencies,' the centripetal (i.e. forces of unity) and centrifugal (i.e. forces of difference)" (p. 25). The self may be constituted as a result of the fusion of these forces, i.e. the simultaneous need to connect with and separate from the other. It is this interplay between the opposing forces (centripetal and centrifugal), which creates contradiction and difference and brings about a dialectical voice. Bakhtin (1986) was a critic of Hegelian-Marxist "dialectics" in the following way: "Take a dialogue and remove the voices (the partitioning of voices), remove the intonations (emotional and individualizing ones), carve out abstract concepts and judgments from living words and responses, cram everything into one abstract consciousness---and that's how you get dialectics" (p. 147).

Dialectical tension is produced as a result of the friction between what appear to be contradictory or opposite phenomena. "Hegelian dialectic" is an argument that posits a thesis and antithesis (point-counterpoint), which are then resolved through a synthesis. A dialectical tension can take many forms. As an example, let's take the tension between blacks and whites, Christianity and Islam, and public and private. The events that are currently occurring in the Middle East may be a result of dialectical tension.

Baxter and Montgomery (1996) find their own dialectical voice based on the actual and imagined dialogues with scholars such as Bakhtin. They highlight several key themes borrowed from Bakhtin's work on dialogism, from which to formulate their own emerging meaning of social and relational dialectics. "These themes reverberate with Bakhtin's notion of 'dialogue' as enacted communication, 'dialogue' as centripetal—centrifugal flux, 'dialogue' as chronotopic, and 'dialogue' as distinct from 'monologue'" (p. 42).

23

Baxter and Braithwaite (2008) comment:

> The central proposition of 'relational dialectics theory' (RDT) is that all of communication is rife with the tension-filled struggle of competing discourses—the discursive oppositions of sociality. An analysis of communication framed by RDT seeks to understand this dialectical process by (a) identifying the various discourses that are directly or indirectly invoked in talk to render utterances understandable and legitimate, and (b) asking how those discourses interpenetrate one another in the production of meaning (Baxter & Braithwaite, 2008, pp. 352-353)

In an interesting analysis of the interpenetration of discourses, the authors use the expressions "synchronic" and "diachronic" to describe the emergence of meaning in dialogue. Diachronic means occurring over time, while the former is taken to mean a single moment in time. Even though meanings may appear to be fixed at any given moment in time, they may also be fluid and changing in the next. Participants may jointly reinforce an old meaning or simply construct a brand new meaning in an ongoing process of production or reproduction. The authors believe that it is this interpenetration of competing discourses that constitutes social reality. Bakhtin (writing as Voloshinov, 1973, p-85) believed that it is not experience that organizes expression, but the other way round—expression organizes experience. The relational dialectics theory (RDT) is unique in that it is the articulation of the "tensionality of difference" as a mechanism that constitutes reality (Baxter, 2006). This process of constitution involves a decentering of the sovereign self that Keats may have referred to in his own way as the annulment of the self. It is through multiple perspectives on the same phenomena, as studied in different contexts, that we may be able to derive meaning through convergence and divergence.

The literature that I have reviewed informs negative capability in some way and points to one thing—being in an ephemeral state of not knowing, ambiguity, and liminality all call for holding and managing dialectical tension over time, and are characterized by different, often contradictory ways of thinking about something. We may experience dialectical tension when our worldview includes two seemingly contradictory (not necessarily dissimilar or unrelated) thoughts, or at least competing ways of thinking about a given topic with no real way to resolve the problem. Some examples of dialectical tension are:

-Group members' struggle between wanting process and content

-Autonomy (abstraction) vs. intimacy

-Togetherness vs. separateness

-Privacy vs. disclosure

-Introversion vs. extroversion

-Emotion vs. cognition

Leaders are often called upon paradoxically to hold very conflicting and often-painful dialectical tensions that cannot be easily resolved and may leave us emotionally and psychologically paralyzed if left unmanaged. Like a state of liminality, we are not fully vested in either polarity. We are at both ends at the same time. It would like standing at the edge of the boundary that separates the two positions, and yet fully taking up one position means giving up the other; and what makes this quandary even more difficult is that both positions are somehow interrelated, not mutually exclusive, even though at first they might appear to be.

I see dialectical tension as the common thread that runs through the bodies of literature that I have been discussing, and yet, this tension resides as subtle nuances in each discipline. A practicing Buddhist who is in a state of mindful awareness and reflective inaction might experience the tension differently from an adult learner. A psychoanalyst, who by virtue of training and expertise holds the dialectical tension with a patient, might experience it very differently from a poet or an organizational consultant. I was interested in contextually understanding how these subtle nuances contribute to the lived experience of participants.

In his 1939 monograph on "negative capability," Bate (2012) discusses disinterestedness, passiveness, sympathy, impersonality, and annulment of the self as key elements. While most scholars who are familiar with Keats's literary genius, would support Bate, I have often wondered if there isn't something radically important that has been overlooked in the literature. As an organizational consultant who has done some work with Keat's ideas over the past 10 years, it has been my experience and that of other colleagues whom I have worked with, that negative capability represents a quandary---a rather perturbed and conflicted frame of mind that may be steeped in dialectics.

A search for the expression negative capability on several academic sites, including the Fielding library of journals and dissertations, returned several pages primarily featuring the work of scholars in organizational psychodynamics and articles critiquing the Keatsian construct in poetry. As the search was narrowed to include the expressions "psychoanalysis" and "Buddhism," a plethora of resources was found that make references to the construct.

As I previously discussed, negative capability is not a mainstream expression that everyone is familiar with. People relate to it in different ways and may think of it as containment, refrain, mindful awareness, reflective inaction, and liminality to name a few. Even Keats, after having used the expression only once, subsequently thought of it as diligent indolence, disinterestedness, annulment of the self, and restless imagination---all of which may suggest an openness to sensation and feeling, the ability to transcend rationality, and the rejection of epistemological bounds.

Poetry

I turn to Keats's famous letter to his brothers George and Thomas Keats in 1817, in which he first coined the expression "Negative Capability." Keats writes:

> At once it struck me what quality went to form a Man of Achievement, especially in literature, and which Shakespeare possessed so enormously---I mean Negative Capability, that is when a man is capable of being in uncertainties, mysteries, doubts, without any irritable reaching fact and reason---Coleridge, for instance would let go by a fine isolated verisimilitude caught from the Penetralium of mystery, from being incapable of remaining content with half-knowledge (Keats, 1817).

In his critical essay on Keats's construct, Bate (1963) deconstructs the poet's famous sentences and suggests that words are at best a "wager of thought," and that what we need is to be openly imaginative with a heightened receptivity to reality, which may involve negating and nullifying one's ego (Bate, 1963). Keats, writing about his dear friend Dilke further comments, "he was a Man who cannot feel he has a personal identity unless he has made up his Mind about every thing. The only means of strengthening one's intellect is to make up one's mind about nothing---to let the mind be a thoroughfare for all thoughts" (Keats, 1817).

It is both ironic and intriguing that a young poet in his early twenties living in the age of romanticism in England with far more renowned poets such as Wordsworth, Shelley, and Coleridge, should have coined such a powerful expression in a moment of intense speculation and imagination. What is particularly audacious, albeit enviable about Keats is the courageous manner in which he not only compares the quality of his own work with Shakespeare's, but also condemns his senior peers. One can only imagine the agonizing risk of challenging the authority of well-established contemporaries of his time, and the enormous inner conflict that Keats may have experienced. His open ambivalence around Wordsworth is just one example of the strife of a young poet trying to find his place under the sun.

In order to understand the essence of Keats's thought, it is important to further deconstruct what he may have implied when he used the famous sentence: "I mean Negative Capability, that is when a man is 'capable' of being in uncertainties, mysteries, doubts, without any 'irritable' reaching fact and reason" (Keats, 1817). I have added single quotes in the above sentence around the two key words by Keats, capable and irritable. As Bate interprets, it is not as though uncertainties and mysteries are being preferred for their own sake. It is our capacity to stay with those uncertainties, while resisting the irritable tendency to extend our identities and half-knowledge in order to resolve them which seems to be key (Bate, 1964).

Bush (1937) writes: "If Shakespeare was always the deity in Keats's poetic heaven, Wordsworth and Milton were saints under the throne. Shakespeare was the very opposite of the egotistical sublime, the great exemplar of negative capability, of undogmatic, unobtrusive, impersonal art, but Wordsworth and Milton were more approachable and more imitable" (Bush, 1937, p- 23). Bush refers to Keats's vacillating allegiance to the two poets as the source of the conflict within himself. His changing positions, attitudes, and fluctuating moods all speak to the existential mysteries and

27

anguish that so mentally occupied him through much of his life. I suggest that these notable idiosyncrasies may have been the source of much dialectical tension between idealism and realism. He constantly struggles to reconcile those dimensions within himself and his work.

It seems clear that Keats's growing interest in the ideal of disinterestedness, thoughts of humility, and openness to amplitude emerges in part from the work of Wordsworth and his own weariness with his peers who "make one start" without "making one feel" (Bate, 1964). His growing disillusionment with their fashions and mannerisms and his deep interest in the "impersonality of genius" and "receptivity" are further illuminated in the following passage:

> It has been an old Comparison for our urging on—the Bee hive—however it seems to me that we should rather be the flower than the Bee…Now it is more noble to sit like Jove tha{n} to fly like Mercury—let us not therefore go hurrying about and collecting honey-bee like, buzzing here and there impatiently from a knowledge of what is to be arrived at: but let us open our leaves like a flower and be passive and receptive—budding patiently under the eye of Apollo and taking hints from every noble insect that favors us with a visit (Keats: Bate, 1964, p-59).

In addition to disinterestedness, "diligent indolence" is also attributed to Keats. It does not imply passivity or deadness, but rather an active imagination. His use of impersonality of genius especially in literature should not be taken to mean a form of depersonalization. On the contrary, his feelings and emotions remain strong. Be it in his poems or Odes, Keats writes with an intensity that would not be possible if he was devoid of strong feelings. The paradox is quite evident, as is Keats's constant vacillation, a struggle between who he is at the core and what he strives to achieve in his rather short-lived career as a poet. I see this as an example of dialectical thinking. He never truly achieves this balance. And it is in these periods of enormous conflict, despair, even depression that he writes some of his finest work. He has the capacity to snap out of his state of glooming reverie, as quickly as he succumbs to it. All it ever takes is his extremely vivid imagination, his "synesthetic imagery," and his love of simplicity in nature to quickly pull him out of whatever state that he finds himself in.

At the suggestion of his friend Benjamin Bailey in 1817, about the time that he begins his famous poem "Endymion" and writes the negative capability letter to his brothers, he is introduced to the work of Hazlitt. In that work, the author refutes the claims of Thomas Hobbes and his eighteenth century followers that all human actions spring forth from an egocentric self-love. Keats is so captivated by the concept, especially Hazlitt's work on disinterestedness that he decides to attend his lectures at the Surrey Institution barely three weeks after he writes the "negative capability" letter to his brothers. Contrary to the claim of "Hobbists" that everything that we do is to help ourselves in some way or to avoid future pain, Hazlitt (1805) writes "I can abstract myself from my present being and take an interest in my future being [only] in the same sense and manner, in which I can go out of myself entirely and enter into the minds and feelings of others" (Hazlitt, 1805).

This capacity for imaginative identification, and the natural disinterestedness of the mind is not to suggest that most people are apathetic and disinterested. The author is emphasizing instead the capacity to lose one's personal identity in some object dearer to ourselves, such that we are able to dissolve our ego in order to understand another. Keats was so influenced by Hazlitt's work that he attended all but one of his lectures. He was captivated by the notion of a "characterless poet," not to be confused with a lack of character per se but a lack of identity.

Keats writes, "What shocks the virtuous philosopher, delights the cameleon poet" and further adds that "a Poet is the most unpoetical of anything in existence because he has no identity—he is continually in for and filling some other body" (Keats, 1817). His notion of the "chameleon poet" (spelled "cameleon" by Keats) has been extrapolated to the field of leadership where references are now made to "chameleon leaders" as those who possess some of the same traits that Keats discusses.

Before moving on to other bodies of literature where conversations are taking place on negative capability, I want to make some closing comments. The words "negative" and "capability" make up the expression "negative capability" and seem to be mutually exclusive; an oxymoron. They cancel out each other and yet, if you examine the words in a more nontraditional light, "negative" does not necessarily mean lack of and the word "positive" does not imply the opposite of negative. The two words are at an odd juxtaposition, which makes the construct so compelling. They are interdependent and complementary, not necessarily opposed; however, this unique relationship is not immediately evident. It is at once apparent that Keats's own painful struggles and tragedies over a very short-lived career, paradoxically may have also accounted for his tremendous brilliance as a poet. In a moment of great speculation and spontaneity, he coins the expression which is now gradually emerging in fields outside of poetry and literature, even as diverse as management, conflict resolution, theater, and transformative learning.

Paradoxical thinking

In her posthumous study, Elson (2010) investigates "levels phenomena" as they relate to paradoxes and develops a cross-contextual definition of "levels of abstraction." Grounding her work in the theories of Korzybski (1933) on consciousness of abstracting and Bateson's (1972a, 1974) appropriations of Russell's theory of logical type and his own double bind theory, Elson takes us on a unique journey inside and outside the field of media ecology which was the thrust of her life's work. While she never directly makes reference to "negative capability," I find many parallels between her work and Keats's construct, especially as they relate to the fields of interpersonal communication and "relational dialectics."

Elson writes:

In human communication, a simple, literal message is rare. It is a virtual axiom of communication theory that messages are complex and multileveled. At very least, every message has a content aspect and a relationship aspect, which classifies the content and is therefore a meta-communication about how content is to be interpreted. Meta-communications help create meanings; however, they also help create ambiguities and paradoxes (Elson, 2010 p-77).

The content and relationship aspects of a message, Elson posits, are not definable in time and space because they exist at different "levels of abstraction."

Elson's work is particularly germane to a hermeneutic understanding of phenomena. The "levels phenomenon" theorized by Elson may add something significant to our existing understanding of paradoxes. Of all the paradoxes that Elson (2010) discusses, such as the "liar's paradox," the "prediction paradox," the "uncertainty paradox," and the "prisoner's dilemma," her analysis of the "double-bind theory" is most notable. She writes: "A communication (what is said) and a meta-communication (the relationship aspect of what is said), differ in ways not definable in terms of time and space. They are of different levels of abstraction" (p-77). The message content can therefore conflict with the message relationship, contributing to dialectical tension. In readily understood paradoxes such as a choice between two orders: STOP and NO STOPPING ANYTIME, one can discern and choose to follow one over the other. In a "double bind," however, such as a sign that says IGNORE THIS SIGN, the choice to comply or not is only an illusion because no matter what, one will disobey the sign anyway and is quite helpless to do anything about it. It is interesting to explore how "double binds" operate in dialectics and interpersonal communication.

As I conducted interviews and analyzed and interpreted data, understanding the relationship between the communication and meta-communication was helpful.

Entanglements and transmedial thinking

In a somewhat paradoxical departure from its intended meaning, Chow (2012) views entanglements as not necessarily emanating from proximity and closeness. She asks, "What kinds of entanglements might be conceivable through partition and partiality rather than conjunction and intersection, and through disparity rather than through equivalence?" (p-2). From such convolutions, she challenges us to think of them as out-foldings superimposed on in-foldings and points us to scientific inquiry in quantum physics which looks at entanglements as mysterious connections between particles which are a result of reactions not attributable to proximity.

This is a compelling notion and brings to mind how contradiction, divergent thinking, and paradox---all the things that we traditionally associate with dissent and disagreement may actually become the identificatory means of connecting with others in discourse and dialogue. From a sociological perspective as well, this form of autonomy may be viewed as emerging from a high level of "social reflexivity" which may be seen as yet another form of entanglement.

Giddens (1987), discussing the implications of the "double hermeneutic" suggests, "nothing confirms more completely the importance of a dialogical model, for only such a model incorporates the attention to reflexivity" (p-48). Chow (2012) cites epic writer Doblin's idea of using a pair of scissors for cutting a narrative into pieces, with each piece continuing to have a life of its own. I consider "negative capability" to be an epic construct. There are so many of what appear to be different, but related, even disjointed pieces (from various contexts) that appear to be in contradiction, and yet you can quickly piece them together in a montage which brings to life the centrality of Keats's concept.

Communicative space

The work of Greenwood and Levin (1998) addresses the use of a skill that is very similar to "negative capability" and germane to the field of organizational development. The authors write:

> Good action science practice focuses heavily on group process skills. In the interventions we have observed by some action scientists, we have been impressed by certain skills they develop. For one thing, they are very patient and persistent with the processes. The calm, persistent, clear, and supportive role that interveners play does much to create the space in which the kind of action science inquiry leading to changes in group process can be developed. Another important feature of action science intervention is the way in which practitioners learn not to feel threatened by silences and vacuums in group processes. Rather than rushing in to fill awkward spaces with sound and action, they keep uncomfortable spaces open longer, confronting the participants with the need to examine their actions in part out of the discomfort caused by the process of standing still (Greenwood & Levin, 1998, p. 201).

For leaders in particular, many of who follow the principles of good action science, the concept of communicative space is critical and I find that negative capability can play a significantly important role in how the work between them and their local stakeholders gets underway, especially at the very initial stages before more enduring relationships can form. The negative space may allow for new thoughts and feelings to openly surface and can then be contained for the sake of the work by both sides, in a manner that increases trust and enhances collaboration.

Given the complexity of the topic and its abstract and paradoxical nature, it was important to select a methodology that honors novelty and creativity. After considering several approaches within the wider field of phenomenology, the "Interpretative Phenomenological Analysis (IPA) methodology was chosen. I discuss it in the following chapter.

CHAPTER THREE
Research Method, Design, and Methodology

Unlike the natural science that studies objects of nature, human science inquiry is about the study of persons or beings that have consciousness. van Manen, (1990) writes: "Phenomenological research is the study of lived experience. It is seeing the world without taxonomizing, classifying, or abstracting it. It does not test hypotheses or theories, but offers plausible insights" (van Manen, 1990, p. 9).

Before I delineate the purpose, methodology, and design of this phenomenological study, it may be important to revisit the research question. I restate the question as follows:

What is it like for leaders to be in a state of negative capability during periods of uncertainty and conflict in the workplace?

What I hope to investigate in this study is how leaders working in a particular context, make sense of their past experiences in the workplace. My question referred to a leader's negative capability frame of mind in the face of organizational pressures and anxiety when the wisdom of refrain is in conflict with the pressure to react. My assumption was that a person is unable to reflect on lived experience without living through that experience. van Manen (1990) suggests that "phenomenological reflection is not introspective, but retrospective" (van Manen, 1990, p. 11). It is a recall.

Interpretative Phenomenological Analysis (IPA): History, origin, and theoretical foundations:

Developed in the mid 90's by Smith et al. (2009), the methodology rests on three major theoretical pillars, a) phenomenology b) hermeneutics, and c) idiography which are briefly discussed in this section in the context of two case studies and subsequently highlighted theoretically. Traditionally deployed in the field of health psychology, and to a smaller extent in clinical settings, the approach is fast gaining popularity and making its way into social science research. I will hereinafter refer to the methodology with the acronym "IPA." I have used the words approach and methodology interchangeably. In order to better understand the epistemological assumptions of IPA and how the approach can be deployed to study negative capability, I present below, two studies

(IPA 1 and 2) conducted by other scholars who researched the lived experiences of participants.

IPA Study 1: Building Connections: An Interpretative Phenomenological Analysis of Qualitative Research Students' Learning Experiences

The study examined the lived experiences of students learning qualitative research in a variety of fields. The authors of the study, Cooper, Fleischer, and Cotton (2012) suggest, "understanding the student experience of learning qualitative research holds important implications for developing effective curricula, improving instructional methods, and enhancing pedagogical theory related to qualitative research" (p. 1).

In reviewing the existing literature on the learning experiences of qualitative research students, the authors discovered that in the past, instructors had only conducted studies with their own students within a particular field or institution. They discovered a gap in the research and undertook the study to examine the lived experience of students from other fields and institutions as well. They were interested in a phenomenological understanding of what it was like for students to study qualitative research in several different contexts, which is a form of triangulation.

"Phenomenology" is an attempt to understand the true meaning and essence of experiences as recounted by participants. In doing phenomenology, one is immersing in the life world of the participants and reliving their experiences or rethinking the actors' thoughts, consistent with the philosophical tradition known as "Verstehen." It also involves setting aside (bracketing) assumptions, biases, and judgments that may otherwise impede the data collection process. In this particular study, the authors decided to delegate the task of conducting interviews to their three research assistants, while they independently conducted the analysis. This is an atypical approach to data collection in IPA, possibly undertaken in order to eliminate unwanted bias and subjectivity, given the unequal status of professors and students.

Semi-structured in-depth interviews were conducted in the IPA tradition with six participants who had no previous ties to the researchers. Data collected by the research assistants were then transcribed and shared with the authors for analysis, who then immersed themselves in the data by reading and re-reading the transcripts several times. The process involved moving from the "idiographic" (particular) interpretation of

35

individual cases to group-level data. This is an example of the "hermeneutic circle" where the analyst is making sense of parts in relation to the whole, and the whole in relation to its parts. It is through this reiterative process of going back and forth, that a hermeneutic understanding of the phenomenon may be achieved.

The researchers Cooper, Fleischer, and Cotton (2012) identified 5 primary themes: a) a variety of feelings are experienced, b) a pivotal experience serves as a catalyst in the learning process, c) the central role of story, d) active learning, and e) relating knowledge to prior knowledge. The literature was consistent with the findings, in that the students learning qualitative research found it to be a very emotional experience. They seemed to experience excitement when they gained real research experience as opposed to understanding it academically. Experiential learning played an important role and was considered to be pivotal to their growth.

One of the challenges faced by the authors was that the research assistants who conducted the interviews were all doctoral students learning qualitative research at the university. A process of "bracketing" was used, whereby the assistants set aside their own assumptions and preconceived notions while conducting the interviews.

The authors' findings indicate that the participants reported a great deal of anxiety at the data collection and analysis stages, which later gave way to renewed excitement and energy during pivotal moments. Some participants experienced those "triggering" moments as epiphanies that enriched their learning process. The literature suggests that students, who have had prior training in quantitative research and the scientific method, report cognitive dissonance as they engage in qualitative research. The authors strongly recommend that instructors in qualitative research should incorporate experiential learning early on in the teaching process, as opposed to relying on theory and epistemology.

IPA Study 2: Self-initiated Expatriates: An Interpretative Phenomenological Analysis of Professional Female Expatriates

Fitzgerald and Howe-Walsh (2008) conducted the study. They examined the experiences of female professionals who expatriated to the Cayman Islands of their own volition. Of the 10 women recruited, 4 dropped out of the study. The participants represented the UK, New Zealand, and the Philippines (an example of triangulated

36

contexts) and occupied positions such as HR Manager, Government Director, Vice President of Finance, and Internal Audit Manager (triangulated roles). The study explored the lived experience of these women by means of face-to-face interviews conducted on the island, in addition to a preliminary phone call from Ireland. The current literature in the international human relations arena informs the experiences of expatriates who are mostly male. The authors suggest that foreign assignments are a predominantly male domain, with women mostly appearing as spouses of expatriates. Therefore the study addressed an important gap in the literature.

The following research questions were posed: a) what influences female professionals to choose a self-initiated international work experience? b) How do the overseas work experiences of professional female self-initiated expatriates affect their perceptions of their future career and employability? c) Do self-initiated female expatriates experience discrimination while overseas? These are examples of open-ended phenomenological questions, which attempt to access the lived experience of participants. The essence of the experience in all its richness is often elusive and discovered by remaining open to surprise, without seeking an outcome.

The literature reveals that historically very few women have been given opportunity for advancement in their careers through foreign placements. Gender and personality differences between men and women have also been cited as possible reasons for precluding women from employment overseas. Multinational Companies (MNCs) typically ignore the human resources aspect of their operations that would address gender equality, and instead focus on other functions more important to the business. It is suggested that the dismally low number of women expatriates in senior positions overseas is a gender-related issue, not an assignment-related problem.

Data were collected by means of semi-structured interviews with participants, initially by telephone from Ireland, followed by face-to-face meetings on the Cayman Islands. Interview transcripts were produced and read and re-read by the researchers with special emphasis on the idiographic accounts. The IPA approach to analysis included developing a thematic network to identify all commons themes and a two-step hermeneutic process where the researcher made sense of the participant's interpretation of the phenomenon (double hermeneutic). A comprehensive case-by-case analysis was conducted on each transcript and involved moving from description to interpretation. A general listing of all themes was completed, followed by a clustering of themes. From the latter, a master table of superordinate themes was created.

The authors report the following findings:

Choosing expatriation

The participants reported several factors that prompted them to leave for an overseas assignment, with their careers being a highly influential factor. The location of the island also was important to them because they wanted to maintain a certain lifestyle that they were used to in London.

Facing challenges

Several participants reported work stress as one of the biggest challenges with working on the island. They were so used to working in London that it was difficult for them to adjust to the new culture and environment. They felt that the work pace was a lot slower, contributing to a lot of additional stress. Two participants who were from the Philippines, reported that the work culture in their country was very different from what they observed on the island. Also, working with a multitude of nationalities posed challenge to them. Other reasons cited were the high cost of living, the division between the locals and the expatriates, and difficulty with forming deep relationships.

Discrimination

While there was not much overt discrimination, the participants felt it nonetheless on account of working within an "old boys network." They felt excluded and adjusted to the feelings of exclusion by working harder and using their knowledge and expertise to get ahead. They also felt that "expatriate discrimination" existed and was subtly promoted by the Government of Cayman Islands through their policies toward expatriates. There was always the fear that their work permits might be revoked if they spoke up.

Value of international experience

Five of the 6 participants reported that they were pleased with their professional growth and the new skills that they had acquired working internationally. They considered these to be valuable additions to their CVs. Their general confidence too had improved considerably.

Despite the challenges that the women faced on account of their work pressures and expatriate identity, they were generally pleased with living and working on the island and considered the experience to be valuable.

IPA studies 1 and 2 are examples of the kind of detailed in-depth analysis that is possible when the researcher is working with a smaller corpus of 6-7 participants. While the outlines presented here do not portray the true depth and particularity of the studies, the reader will find those elements to be true in the actual work. While both studies are individually unique, they do provide a general overview of the thoroughness and integrity of the IPA approach to studying phenomena. The approach is built on the following theoretical pillars:

Phenomenology

Husserl (1970), Heidegger (1971, 1977, 1999), Merleau-Ponty (1962, 1974), and Sartre (1948) are prominent philosophers whose work has made a significant contribution to the field. As founder of the philosophical school of phenomenology, Husserl broke from the positivist tradition and is credited with the development of "phenomenological reduction" (epoche), also known as "bracketing". In understanding the essence of a phenomenon, Husserl believed that it is important to distinguish it from "noumenon." In bracketing something, we are trying to understand the true essence of a phenomenon, while setting aside our own assumptions, beliefs, and judgments about it. It would be like peeling away the layers of an onion and trying to understand its core—a form of unpacking.

Smith, Flowers & Larkin (2009) discuss Husserl's thinking as focusing on experience and perception. They write: "In developing Husserl's work further, Heidegger, Merleau-Ponty, and Sartre each contribute to a view of the person as embedded and immersed in a world of objects and relationships, language and culture, projects and concerns" (Smith, Flowers & Larkin, 2009, p. 21). They move us from Husserl's position towards a more interpretive and perspectival involvement in experience, which invokes a lived process.

Hermeneutics

"Hermeneutics" is the theory of interpretation. It is sometimes used interchangeably with the term "exegesis." The latter refers primarily to the interpretation of text, while the former is a wider discipline that includes all forms of communication: written, verbal, and non-verbal. Modern "hermeneutics" has also come to include "semiotics" (the study of signs and sign processes). Schleiermacher (1998) writes:

> Interpretation depends on the fact that every person, besides being an individual themself, has receptivity for all other people. But this itself seems only to rest on the fact that everyone carries a minimum of everyone else within themself, and divination is consequently excited by comparison with oneself. (Schleiermacher, 1998 pp. 92-93)

One of the major theorists in the field has been Heidegger whose aim was to make the case for a hermeneutic phenomenology. In trying to interpret the nature of our being, Heidegger believed that things have both a visible (manifest) and tacit (hidden) meaning for us, which may very well be the true essence of phenomenology. In trying to examine something that may be latent or disguised, I tried to come to terms with my own unknowing in this study.

In his important work Heidegger (1962) explicitly discusses his theory of interpretation (which was a departure from Husserl's predominantly descriptive phenomenology) and writes: "Whenever something is interpreted as something, the interpretation will be founded essentially upon the—fore-conception. An interpretation is never a pre-suppositionless apprehending of something presented to us" (Heidegger, 1962, pp. 191-192). This is to suggest that the participants, readers, and investigators all bring their pre-conceptions to a study, including their unique assumptions to an encounter and therefore make sense of that episode as they view it through their own experiential lenses. While I had no control over the pre-conceptions of participants, I did try to bracket my own assumptions during the study.

Smith, Flowers & Larkin (2009) comment: "Indeed a consideration of Heidegger's complex and dynamic notion of fore-understanding helps us see a more enlivened form of bracketing as both a cyclical process and as something which can only be partially achieved. In fact this connects with reflexive practices in qualitative psychology" (Smith, Flowers & Larkin, 2009 p. 25).

Gadamer (1990) is yet another important theorist in hermeneutics. He emphasizes the importance of history and tradition in the interpretive process. He believes that the phenomenon (the thing itself) may influence the interpretation, which in turn can influence the fore-structure, which can then influence the interpretation itself. When I read and interpreted the text, I was in a sense, having a dialogue with what was old (a fore-understanding) and what was new (the text).

Hermeneutic circle

This is not an idea that is attributed to any theorist in particular. It is something that most hermeneutic writers subscribe to. To put it simply, a "hermeneutic circle" is a dynamic relationship that exists between a part and the whole. To understand a part, you look to the whole, and to understand the whole, you must be able to understand its parts. While analyzing data, I was intermittently looking at parts of the text in relation to the whole and the whole as it related to its parts.

Dilthey (1979) suggests, "that for us to know what a polar bear is like someone must have seen one, but how could he ever know that he had seen a polar bear unless he knew what they were like? We cannot pinpoint the meaning of a word unless we read it in its context" (Dilthey, 1979, p. 130). Dilthey believed that man is incapable of stepping outside his own experience and can only disentangle from that experience. It is this circularity of knowledge that Dilthey also referred to as the "hermeneutic circle."

Verstehen

Philosophers and classical thinkers such as Dilthey (1979) have embraced the doctrine of "Verstehen." Martin (2000) writes: "In its strongest forms, "Verstehen" entails reliving the experience or at least rethinking the actor's thoughts, while in its weaker forms, it only involves reconstructing the actor's rationale for acting" (p-1). It is also known as the interpretive or participatory investigation of social phenomena. It is central to the rejection of positivist social science. It is beyond the scope of this study to get into a full-length discussion of "Verstehen," but it is however important to offer two contemporary interpretations of Dilthey's central notions.

Martin (2000) comments on the reliving interpretation of Dilthey's position:

1. In order to understand human beings, it is important to empathize with them.
2. In order to empathize with them, it is necessary to relive their experience (Martin, 2000, p-11).

While Dilthey did not believe that it was important to relive the experiences of individuals or even empathize with them in order to understand, he did however believe in the reconstruction of thoughts and feelings manifested in their actions. Therefore Dilthey's position based on the reconstruction of thoughts and feelings may be restated as follows:

1. In order to understand human beings it is necessary to reconstruct the inner life of these human beings from its manifestation in their actions

2. This reconstructing involves knowing what the inner lives of these human beings are" (Martin, 2000 p-12).

Idiography

The "idiographic" approach to research has to do with the particular. Contrasted with the "nomothetic" approach that is antithetical and predominantly quantitative; often dealing with generalization that applies to broader populations, "idiography" is about "particularity." This study is a rich account of how participants made sense of particular experiences and phenomena, in addition to a detailed narrative of the textual analysis of those experiences. The idiographic approach adopted in the study dealt with particular people making sense of particular phenomena in particular contexts. It was an inductive and purposive approach.

Epistemological considerations of IPA

Despite its growing popularity, IPA continues to be a misunderstood methodology in the field of qualitative psychology. Hefferon and Gil-Rodriguez (2011) contend that research students tend to choose the approach prior to fully understanding its epistemological foundation and philosophy. At the heart of that philosophy is quality, and not quantity---less is more. It is not a simple thematic analysis with little emphasis on interpretation. The authors write: "Students consistently appear to experience pressure to include too many participants, seemingly in order to placate research boards and supervisors in line with the quantitative monopoly within academic research. This necessarily deemphasizes IPA's commitment to idiography" (Hefferon & Gil-Rodriguez, 2011, p. 756). They suggest that the larger the corpus, the more descriptive and superficial the analysis. Conversely, a smaller corpus may facilitate a deeper, more in-depth study of the phenomenon. It is easier to compare and contrast themes with 5-6 participants, than it is with a much larger group of say 14-16. A smaller corpus also results in a smaller number of emerging themes, which can then be carefully studied for convergence and divergence.

Pilot study

This is a report on the pilot study that was conducted by means of semi-structured in-depth interviews with three leaders. Two of the participants were senior leaders in business organizations and the third individual was in private practice as a career coach. The purpose of the preliminary study was to develop a framework for the study design and assess whether the question was practically researchable and provided a good foundation for approaching the full dissertation. Interviews were conducted using the protocol and schedule that were already approved by IRB. Data collection included digitally recording the interviews and subsequently transcribing them in numbered transcripts. These transcripts and data analysis were submitted to the supervisor for his review.

The following themes emerged from the first interview: "Dealing with conflict and upheaval," "making sense of corporate politics," "managing competing pressures and deadlines," and "containing others' anxieties." The themes that emerged from the second interview were: "Cautious when facts are scarce and decisive when facts are plenty," "dealing with personal reactivity," "making sense of social conflicts," "managing personal affronts and threats to identity." The following themes emerged from the final interview: "Resolving issues," "introverted leadership style," "discomfort with silence," "dealing with social norms," "holding the tension between reflecting and acting," "wanting closure and certainty," "frozen and immobilized by tension." No common themes emerged from the three interviews.

The participants for the pilot included leaders who not only had previous ties with me, but also were conversant with the topic of the study. In keeping with Murphy's Law, surprises were fully anticipated. With the exception of a few minor interruptions beyond my control, the pilot progressed quite smoothly. In order to protect the identities of the participants who shared rich accounts of their professional lives unreservedly, the interview transcripts did not contain any identifying information that could have put the participants at risk or jeopardy. All transcripts contained highlighted text where I could identify key areas for consideration and further exploration. Data from the pilot interviews were not included in this study.

Results of the pilot

Conducting the pilot interviews was an edifying experience. It was a prototype that gave me a sense of what it would be like to conduct similar interviews for the dissertation. I remained open to surprise and was fully expecting something to go wrong; however, the interviews progressed quite smoothly. One reason may have been that I knew the participants well, and so there already was a level of trust between us.

Although the pilot study sample was very small, it yielded rich data. It also alerted me to appropriately modify the interview schedule in order to pursue additional questions and delete those that did not add anything significant to the study. As an example, asking leaders how they entered their profession was considered to be an irrelevant line of questioning and was subsequently modified in the interview schedule for the study.

The pilot study revealed that I had wrongly assumed that the participants were familiar with negative capability. During the interviews, I sensed that they found it challenging to think and talk about something so vague. I also discovered that 60 minutes was not a sufficient duration for the interviews. It did not allow enough time to immerse myself in the participants' life worlds. In consultation with the study supervisor, I decided to extend the study interviews to 90 minutes.

Main study design

The three contexts (domains) that I selected for my study were academia, private practice (self employed practitioners), and business organizations. I decided that looking at negative capability from multiple perspectives might add depth and complexity to the study that may not be achieved from individual accounts in a single context.

Smith, Flowers, and Larkin (2009) suggest, "in multi-perspectival studies, the exploration of one phenomenon from multiple perspectives can help the analyst to develop a more detailed and multifaceted account of that phenomenon" (Smith, Flowers, and Larkin, 2009, p. 52). Critics have argued both for and against homogenous sampling. Some believe that recruiting participants with previous sentient ties offers an advantage from the standpoint of perceived safety and openness; others however argue that it takes away from the richness and diversity of the experience. I took the latter position.

Selection criteria and recruitment

The selection criteria were as follows:

1. Participants should be within the age range of 35-65.
2. Should be currently employed (or self-employed in the case of private practitioners) and have at least 5 years experience at their place of work.
3. Be familiar with the notion of "negative capability."
4. Must have experienced or currently experiencing significant anxiety around at least one situation at work where they find themselves in a state of uncertainty and conflict. This is typically an ongoing episode and not a sporadic incident.
5. Must be comfortable sharing their experiences with the researcher in a one-on-one setting.
6. Must agree to sign the informed consent form and be willing to have the conversations digitally recorded.

The following documents were used in the recruitment, selection, and interview processes and appear at the end of this study.

Appendix B: Demographic information gathering form.

Appendix C: Preliminary email inquiry

Appendix D: Participant recruitment letter

Appendix E: Informed consent

Appendix F: Telephone script

Appendix G: Interview schedule (academia, private practice, and business organizations).

The participants were recruited to a purposive sample and drawn from academia, private practice, and business organizations. They had no previous personal or professional ties with me. I had hoped that this triangulation would provide a unique insight into how leaders view negative capability in different contexts.

Data collection

I conducted interviews with 15 leaders. One of the participants subseq withdrew from the corpus. Her data has not been included in the study. With the exception of one interview (case 4) where we ran into last-minute technical difficulties and so had to switch to a teleconference, the remaining interviews were conducted on the Go To Meeting platform with the webcam enabled. The interviews were digitally recorded and had an average duration of 90 minutes each with a few extra minutes allowed for initial setup. Immediately following the interview, I transcribed the digital recordings in order to safeguard the confidentiality of the material and protect the identity of the participants. This sense of immediacy also enabled me to capture the important moments while my recollections of the interview were still fresh. The transcripts were then coded, read, and re-read several times in order to immerse myself in the life world of participants and begin to make sense of the phenomenon.

Appendix G contains the interview schedule that was used. A decision was made to not include the expression negative capability in the interview questions. Even though at the time of recruitment, participants claimed to have a general understanding of the phenomenon, it is not a part of contemporary terminology. The pilot study also indicated that participants might find such a concept a bit challenging. Smith, Flowers, and Larkin (2009) suggest addressing the research question sideways if the topic is very abstract. Accordingly, I emphasized uncertainty and ambiguity throughout the interviews, as opposed to directly addressing negative capability.

Leaders were asked the same questions in all three contexts. My objective in the interview was to not probe the context, but understand what may have been the subtle nuances relevant to a particular context and not others. The schedule was meant to be a facilitator's guide and followed the recommended protocol of IPA, which suggests that the participants not be inundated with too many questions or multiple phenomena.

The complexity and novelty of this method is that the researcher is not expected to be a detached observer, but a participant observer actively involved in the process. I met the participants where they were. On the other hand, I was also wearing the researcher's hat and interpreting how the participants were interpreting the phenomenon. Managing that dialectic was an important part of the interview process.

46

Data management

With each of the 4 transcript readings, the data collected during interviews were coded and recoded; then finally coded as a whole in order to identify any emergent themes and patterns. As a reiterative process, it called for checking and rechecking with the participants' accounts to make sure that what was being recorded is what they intended to convey in the interviews. While I made a deliberate attempt to reflect on the process as it unfolded, some of it was undoubtedly reflexive and out of my own awareness.

A reflexive researcher seeks to analyze the impact of self on the entire process of data collection, analysis, and interpretation (Hammersley & Atkinson, 1990; Steir, 1991). This study is reported in the first person (active voice) as an indication that I was intimately involved in the generation of knowledge, as opposed to being a silent spectator (Steir, 1991; Webb, 1992). Rose & Webb (1998) suggest, "a reflexive researcher does not seek to divide parts of the self from the whole" (Rose & Webb, 1998, p. 556). I was aware that as I conducted the analysis and made interpretations, my multidisciplinary background (which includes psychodynamics, organizational development, and aesthetics) helped shape this process and provided a new repertoire of interpretive skills to draw from. Even as the interviews were conducted, a preliminary process of interpretation and sense making had already begun for me; however, I set aside my own assumptions and preconceptions, so as to keep the interviews focused on the participants' life worlds. This is to be expected in interviews of a qualitative nature where meaning is being jointly constructed by the participant and researcher.

I am aware that my study draws on literature that is both eclectic and multidisciplinary. I approached this work with a sense of excitement, intellectual curiosity, and surprise. I had no preconceived notions that the study participants and myself would view negative capability through the same cognitive lens.

In keeping with the IPA methodology, I conducted a comprehensive textual analysis of the meaning and content of participants' narratives. My concern was not particularly with the prosodic aspects of recordings, even though notes were made during the interviews around discernable patterns and rhythm of the discussion. All data were transcribed in line-numbered transcripts and a detailed semantic record of that data was maintained and shared with the research supervisor only. A line-by line analysis of the experiential claims of participants was conducted using the following protocol suggested by Smith et al. (2009):

1. Identify themes emerging from both convergence and divergence.
2. Have an inner dialogue between what you read in the transcripts and what was coded at the time of interview. A psychological interpretation of concerns around what was being shared by the participants to be noted.
3. Develop a structure that illustrates the relationship between various themes.
4. Turn for assistance to the research supervisor and faculty member who are experienced in narrative analysis and research.
5. Reflect on your own perceptions, paradigms, and biases if any without allowing them to enter the analysis (bracketing).
6. Develop a detailed narrative and commentary, preferably supplemented by visual diagrams, table, or charts.

Analysis and interpretation

Before discussing the data analysis in the following chapter, it is important to note that the analysis was conducted by interpreting the text at two levels. Ricoeur (1970) writes about two kinds of interpretation, using the expression "hermeneutics" to refer to the theory of interpretation:

1. The "hermeneutics of meaning-recollection," which provides a faithful disclosure of the participants' accounts as they make sense of the phenomenon. This is entirely from the perspective of the interviewee with minimal input of the researcher and can take the form of descriptive text including short quotes, metaphors, symbols and other content extracted from the transcripts.

2. The "hermeneutics of suspicion" may involve going below the surface and often behind the phenomenon being studied, in order to understand and interpret its deeper meaning. The researcher conducting this level of analysis tries to make sense of the phenomenon from the participants' accounts, as the participants are making sense of the phenomenon from their own

standpoint. This is known as the "double hermeneutic." In order to dig deeper into the life world of the participant, it is often necessary to take an unconventional approach that is not typically grounded in the data. Psychoanalysis is a good example of going against the grain and interpreting meaning at an unconscious and irrational level. Given that this study involved researching the negative capability phenomenon sideways and not directly, the "hermeneutics of suspicion" gave me an opportunity to understand core aspects of the phenomenon that may not have been otherwise possible.

Jerpbak (2006) suggests that a hermeneutic phenomenologist will not limit "circling" to interview texts alone. The lived experience of a phenomenon is drawn from multiple sources. I argue that when narratives are co-constructed by a participant and researcher, their interpretations too are grounded in more than just the content of the conversations. They are sometimes the result of the paradigmatic framework, worldviews, and contexts in which we are embedded. These interpretations may come from outside the interview and are just as important to analysis as those that are grounded in text. While I attempted as far as possible to stay within the confines of data that were generated, some interpretations were not directly related to the data, but inform the study. Moving forward, the interviews will be referred to as "cases." While analyzing data from the transcripts, I asked myself the following questions:

- What was the participant saying (both manifestly and tacitly)?

- What was the participant feeling and emoting?

- What fears and anxieties were being expressed or held back?

- What was the participant evoking in me (countertransference)?

Reasons for deploying IPA in the study

1. Given the nature of the topic and my focus on interpretive research, I decided that an open-ended semi-structured interview would work well as it allows room for free association. It is purposive and directive without being intrusive. In "symbolic

interactionism" (Prus, 1996), the researcher is not a hands-off observer, but is an active participant himself. He is intersubjectively influencing and is being influenced by research participants, as they collectively construct a shared meaning of reality.

2. Smith et al. (2009) approach is idiographic, in that it attempts to understand the essence and meaning of contingent, novel, and subjective phenomena. Unlike natural sciences that take a nomothetic approach, the focus was not to generalize or describe objective phenomena.

3. The hermeneutic phenomenological focus of this methodology was particularly suited for my study because it is the explication of experiential meanings that people attach to their life events. It is not a biographical account or a validation of what they have lived. As Heidegger (1962) would say: "It is the attentive practice of thoughtfulness."

4. In addition to understanding the experience of participants, the interview narratives provided valuable data on the meaning that is attached to that experience.

van Manen (1990) summarizes hermeneutics with the following words that truly capture the essence of the approach: "To do hermeneutic phenomenology is to attempt to accomplish the impossible: to construct a full interpretive description of some aspect of the life world, and yet to remain aware that lived life is always more complex than any explication of meaning can reveal" (van Manen, 1990, p. 18).

Assessing qualitative research

Qualitative research has always been the subject of criticism, mostly from the positivist perspective. Unlike quantitative studies, there are no firm guidelines for what constitutes good qualitative research. Given the reflexive and paradoxically bilateral nature of the role assumed by qualitative researchers, it is even harder to lay down principles.

Yardley (2000) has delineated 4 broad principles for assessing the quality of such research. They are as follows: a) "sensitivity to context" which can take such forms as the awareness of the socio-cultural milieu in which the study is situated, commitment to the idiographic and particular, and good interviewing skills that demonstrate care and empathy, b) "commitment and rigor" implies the commitment made by the researcher to the confidentiality of a participant's account, protection of data, and sensitivity to the feelings and affect of participants. Rigor means the thoroughness with which the research was conducted and the data analyzed. It also implies honoring the guidelines of a particular methodology, while remaining open to emergence and novelty, c) "transparency and coherence" mean describing in detail, each step of the process followed during the recruitment, data collection, and analysis stages. Transparency also suggests that the researcher makes a conscious effort to report in the analysis and discussion chapters, exactly what was discovered, without having to embellish the data or findings. Any challenges and limitations, included "bracketing" must be carefully discussed with the analysis. Coherence of a study, will inevitably be judged by the reader; however the researcher can ensure that the themes and arguments presented are well organized and informed by the extant and emerging literature, and d) "impact and importance" suggests that regardless of the attention and scrutiny given to a study, the "proof of the pudding" lies in whether the reader finds something important or useful in the findings.

IPA meets all 4 of the above criteria for assessment. Since the inception of the methodology in the mid nineties, hundreds of studies have been conducted on a variety of topics. Even though the methodology is rooted in "qualitative psychology" and "hermeneutic phenomenology," it is now being extensively deployed in other areas of social science research. To the best of my knowledge, I am one of the first few researchers at Fielding Graduate University (outside the psychology department) who have conducted doctoral research using IPA.

Assumptions

1. The study assumed that the participants would be able to recall their past experiences and narrate them with some accuracy during the interview. Additionally, they would be willing to share those experiences with me in order to help construct meaning of lived experience.
2. It was assumed that given the obscurity of the expression negative capability outside the realm of poetry and English literature, participants might find it easier to understand and better relate to the experience of uncertainty and paradox.
3. It was assumed that participants have a fair understanding of the topic under investigation.

51

Bracketing assumptions

I bracketed the following assumptions, preconceptions, and biases that may have otherwise impeded the study. This meant consciously assuming a state of negative capability without regard for the doctrinaire of knowledge.

1. Even though the leaders that I recruited from academia, private practice, and business organizations claimed to have a good understanding of negative capability, I had some apprehension, given the obscurity of the construct in everyday life.

2. During various stages of the recruitment cycle, beginning with the initial contact with participants, the email communications (See Appendices C, D, and E) all provided a clear definition of negative capability, including an example of what might constitute it. If certain participants did not understand the topic, further clarifications were offered before selecting them for the study. Despite that initiative, I had some reservation that leaders would be able to clearly articulate how they made sense of the topic.

3. After a decision was made to replace the negative capability expression with other, more familiar words such as uncertainty, ambiguity, and perplexity in the interview schedule, I suspected that we might end up researching the conditions, rather than the disposition.

4. Given the large corpus containing 15 in-depth interviews and the enormous volume of data that would be generated, I had some concerns, whether it would be possible to do a thorough case-by-case analysis and penetrate the true essence of negative capability at the descriptive, linguistic, and conceptual levels. My anxiety was in part precipitated by what I had already read in the literature. Smith, Flowers, and Larkin (2009) specifically alert new researchers to not conduct an IPA study involving more than 6 participants. A detailed microanalysis becomes challenging with a larger corpus.

5. Having worked with and experienced negative capability since 2002, I had speculated that most of us are not naturally gifted with that unique disposition. Unlike psychotherapists, psychoanalysts, and psychodynamic consultants who cultivate the negative capability state of mind by undergoing rigorous training as part of their profession, it is not a competency that is typically familiar to leaders.

Areas of research:

I explored the following primary areas of research, as reflected in the interview schedule:

1. Negotiating and managing uncertainty and conflict in the workplace.
2. Living with and holding paradox and ambiguity in 3 contexts: a) academia b) private practice, and c) business organizations.

CHAPTER FOUR
Data Analysis and Interpretation

I begin this report with 14 individual case narratives in order to introduce the reader to the life world of the participant leaders. This is in keeping with the "idiographic" focus of IPA. A group narrative follows the individual cases. Certain cases may appear to be more elaborate than others. I take responsibility for this and while I tried to "bracket" my own assumptions and biases in order to do proper justice to the analysis, I realize that subjectivity plays an important role in hermeneutics. As with many semi-structured interviews of this nature where participants have the freedom to free associate without interruption from the researcher, I too experienced that sometimes the discussions would go off topic and had to be gently steered back. At times, I felt as though the participants were leading me. As far as possible, I have reproduced data that were germane to the study and contributed in some way to an understanding of the topic. Phenomenology is not about faithfully reporting everything, but more importantly, reporting everything that faithfully contributes to developing an understanding of the phenomenon.

The participants' comments are reproduced verbatim. They include words and expressions that were phonetically deciphered from the audio files. In order to protect the integrity of the data, no attempt was made to correct the spelling of any words that may appear to be slang. Here is a list of commonly appearing symbols and punctuation marks and the meanings ascribed to them by the researcher:

(......) means pauses.
(Ummmmm) means that the participant was thinking and reflecting.
(LOL) is an abbreviation for laughter.
I have also made a note of expressions such as "choking" when the interview became too emotionally overwhelming for the participants, possibly because they were sharing painful experiences from the past. When I sensed those moments, I took a pause and reached out to them with empathy.

With each case, I provide themes that emerged from the interviews. These are illustrated with the help of interview extracts (denoted by the letter P). With each theme,

I share my brief interpretations (denoted by the letter R). Following the recommended protocol of IPA, no citations from the extant literature are required with individual case studies. The entire emphasis is on the life world of the participant at this level of analysis. References to literature are made in the "group narrative" that deals with the superordinate themes. As I analyzed the data, I discovered several important connections with theories that I had not previously reviewed. I discuss these in the next chapter.

Following the 14 case narratives, I provide tables 1.2 and 1.3 containing a "clustering of themes" and a "master listing of superordinate themes" for the entire group corpus. These tables are arrived at using data extracted from table 1.1 (following the appendices) that includes an initial random listing of key words, phrases, and expressions used in the interviews. Pseudonyms were used throughout the study and identifying information that may potentially put a participant at risk was not disclosed. Finally, a group narrative appears at the end of the chapter.

Case 1: Amanda (Private practice)

Amanda is a highly articulate independent consultant of British origin who lives in the US with her husband and children and works predominantly with high-end clients in the healthcare industry. She is a certified coach who seems greatly influenced by the work, thinking, and methodology of Kegan and associates.

The first half of the interview dealt with her personal, rather than professional issues. Clearly these issues were most pressing and foremost on her mind at the time of the interview. She is struggling with serious mental health issues of her two sons, one of whom suffers from chronic obsessive-compulsive disorder (OCD) and the other with a severe form of anxiety. Both sons are grown, but still live with her. While she feels very competent and qualified to handle even the most challenging issues for her professional clients, she feels utterly helpless, uncertain, and shaky on the home front. Even though Amanda came to the interview extremely composed and confident, the enormous tension that she must feel on account of her personal issues was palpable throughout our conversation. At one point in the interview she commented that dealing with such uncertain and highly painful experiences on the home front makes her the coach that she is today. I found her to be rather stoic and devoid of emotion at certain times during the interview, despite the emotionally laden nature of the discussion. She did not appear bored or disengaged at any time during our interview.

Amanda has taken great pains to get herself educated in OCD, and at the time I recruited her, she had mentioned how she believes that the practice of "negative capability" may well be a very helpful tool to cognitively manage the disease. OCD is a condition that is plagued with recurring uncertainty, not knowing, and the uncontrollable impulsive to quickly disperse into action or rituals as a means of temporarily alleviating the ensuing anxiety. I see this as a topic worthy of further discussion in the next chapter.

During the interview, I pursued the linkages between uncertainty, negative capability, and OCD in order to better understand how Amanda made sense of her state of perplexity that seems to have been exacerbated by the hopelessness of her unique situation. As a leader in private practice, how does one deal with the ever-present threat and danger of having to confront these huge challenges in one's personal life?

Emergent themes: Sense of identity, framing and reframing, intermingling of personal and professional life, obsessive compulsive behavior, levels of consciousness, polarity management, holding the tension

Sense of identity

P: "I don't like to be seen as a self-serving leader. I don't want to be thought of as someone who wants to lead, to be seen, to be validated."

R: This strong "sense of identity" and awareness of how others see her leadership style at work, was a pervasive theme throughout the interview.

Framing and reframing

P: "Yes, to frame problems differently. My style is one that incorporates the wisdom of the group. It is very participative."

R: Framing and reframing was a repetitive theme during the interview. Framing is a set of ideas and assumptions with which we sometimes struggle in order to make sense of the world. They help us construct meaning and are cognitive lenses. Reframing may require the capacity to break free from our self-created frames. As Amanda struggles to hold the paradox between being a mother and a professional, a wife and leader, she uses her framing/reframing skills to negotiate and manage the different roles that she holds.

Intermingling of personal and professional life

When asked to talk about a time that she found it particularly hard to determine (make sense of) certain experiences, Amanda commented: "Absolutely! Not to do with my work, but personal life. Wait!!!! I am just going to check if I am in a place in the home where I can speak openly. Wait a moment." (R: She seemed very guarded and anxious about the situation on her home front). "Okay, so I can. I have to deal with mental health issues in my family. As you can imagine, with mental health, your best tools don't serve you well. You are dealing with things that your mind cannot rationally determine or figure. Right or wrong are irrelevant. How do you manage yourself in the face of extreme stress? I have most definitely been in situations where there was a great deal of chaos. A great deal of emotion...danger where my past tools and experiences were in many ways, of little help to me."

R: Panic, helplessness, confusion, and uncertainty on the one hand and resolute self-control on the other, seemed to describe Amanda's frame of mind during the interview. It was interesting that at the first available opportunity, she chose to talk about her personal issues, rather than professional issues. I decided not to steer her away because I sensed a great deal of urgency and energy around her personal issues. It was important to allow her to express herself before proceeding with the remainder of the interview. The meaning that I make of this is that leaders are sometimes overwhelmed with pressing personal issues that they want to discuss with someone, but must show up at work with full composure. These emotions may be difficult to contain. The organization is not a good enough container for emotions, and this suppressed anxiety may over time contribute to the formation of "social defenses."

Obsessive Compulsive Disorder

P: "So two of my children have had very significant struggle. One was diagnosed with severe OCD. I talked a bit about that when we last spoke. And it's a condition in which the brain gets stuck on certain intrusive thoughts that become rooted. They live with those thoughts and sometimes they come to faulty conclusion that if they do certain rituals they will either manage the anxiety or prevent the feared event from happening. 'My mother is going to die. If I count backward from 100, I can stop it. If I do that, she will be safe.' The secret to getting better is by reframing the fear (it's just the OCD) and enduring it without engaging in the soothing ritual. Because the brain then gets habituated to the fear. Every time you perform the ritual to get rid of the anxiety, you actually make it worse in your neural network in the brain until you break the connections."

R: She seemed very educated about the condition and spoke about it eloquently throughout the interview. Amanda was clearly overwhelmed on account of her son's mental health issues. It was interesting how she passionately discussed the condition and the effort that she had invested into understanding OCD.

P: "When they have the thought and don't perform the ritual, there is absolute terror at first. that space there is absolute terror. It is a life and death situation for them. It's about brain chemistry because if you force yourself to experience the fear and don't perform the ritual, you will gradually feel less fear. You will break the faulty connections that say 'If I do X, Y will happen.'... Neurons that fire together, wire together and OCD is a faulty connection you need to break."

Ritualistic behavior during uncertainty

P: "OCD is a doubting condition. You doubt everything. It is only when you embrace doubt integrally that you can free yourself from it."

R: At this point, I asked Amanda if she saw any commonalties between OCD and the ritualistic behavior in organizations. 'The checking, rechecking, repetition, and rituals can be quite irrational at times, I said to her.'

She commented: "I would not necessarily say it is irrational. It may be irrational from my perspective, not theirs. People are constantly managing their fears in organizations...fear of looking stupid, fear of losing relationships, fear of not progressing etc."

R: It seemed to me as though Amanda had difficulty staying in an inquiry mode. Her mind appeared to be made up about what was happening to her both personally and professionally.

Levels of consciousness (abstraction) and work of Kegan (1994)

P: "So I hesitate using the word OCD about a situation other than a disease. When you know someone who has it, you find the use of OCD for other than disease, insensitive."

"There are repetitive behaviors based on narratives just as OCD is based on narratives. A good coach helps them see narratives they have created and then call them into question. That is the work of Robert Kegan and his work around change. I am certified by Kegan to be a coach, using his approach and it is all about we have a goal but find ourselves going counter to achieving that goal...we dig deeper and find ourselves protecting ourselves from things that might happen if we engage in those behaviors. So what Kegan would say is that the goal is our foot on the gas, but the things we are protecting ourselves from...whatever they may be...are our foot on the brake. We get stuck. Underneath those fears, we find the stories and when we tease apart the stories that maybe served us in the past, we realize that they may be completely false today."

R: Amanda discussed quite vociferously the use of reframing and moving to higher levels of consciousness (abstraction) in order to better understand what was happening at moments of uncertainty and ambiguity. She gave examples from her work with Kegan who has greatly influenced her thinking.

P: "Going from one level of consciousness to the next is about taking the unconscious and making it conscious. Kegan talks about the socialized mind, self-authoring mind, and self-transforming mind. How little we can really control. Control is such an illusion. We cannot change the uncertainty, but only our attitude toward it. I cannot be like some Buddhists who are able to stay with the uncertainty and accept things without wanting to change them. I want to have an impact."

Managing polarities

R: Amanda is a leader who has a good conceptual understanding of negative capability, and so I directly broached the topic with her and inquired how she made sense of the construct. Her response: "It is an approach which is both-and not either-or. My philosophy of leading is not one thing or another—it is keeping people psychologically safe and holding them accountable. There can be tension there---polarity management. American business used to say you can have cost or quality—not both. The Japanese showed that it was a false dichotomy. Manage the polarities and you can come up with a win-win, both-and solutions. Is 'negative capability' a transient stage? Leaders exist to create results and so leaders need not be paralyzed by not knowing. To be able to acknowledge that they don't know, but perhaps use their past experiences to figure out something that might work and try it out. It is comfort with discomfort!!"

R: Quite often it is not a matter of taking an either-or approach to solving problems, but rather asking whether the problem is indeed solvable or if it require holding a paradox and polarities? Amanda shared in the interview that she does not think that there is a resolution on her home front, as it relates to her sons' illness. She seems to have come to terms with her helplessness. All she can do is continue to hold the tension (see the following theme).

Holding the tension of opposites (paradox)

R: When asked what she meant by holding the tension in an uncertain situation, Amanda responds: "Well, so I am talking about different situations, not necessarily holding the tension in the same situation. In a place where I don't act (such as in her personal predicament with her son's illness), that is when I sit with tension because there is to my mind---there is no way to resolve the two oppositions. I just have to manage my feelings about it. It's very difficult---painful and it nags at me, but other than that there are few situations where I cannot see a resolution."

R: This huge dichotomy/dialectic between her personal and professional life and the helplessness that she felt in holding the two polarities was worth noting. I interpreted it as overcompensation on the professional front triggered in part by her acute helplessness on the personal front.

Negative capability

P: "Negative capability is called accepting uncertainty—or embracing uncertainty because it is the need to know (certitude) that drives the behavior. And if you can live with doubt when you have OCD, you can get better. I don't know that if I count from 100 backward that my mother would die. Maybe she will, but parents are not comfortable with letting their children struggle and experience anxiety—they are enablers—they clean the entire house with Lysol; they act as though they themselves have OCD. The importance of not enabling is central—it is absolutely central. Every time you create an illusory safety, you are playing into the problem by running away from uncertainty and not knowing."

R: The interview with Amanda opened a new frontier for exploration. From her account, it did seem that negative capability, in addition to being a cognitive lens through which we can understand leaders, might also be a unique cognitive tool that can be used to help alleviate the suffering of OCD patients. I discuss this in the next chapter.

Case 2: Benjamin (private practice)

Benjamin is an independent organizational consultant in private practice. He lost his wife to cancer after 35 years of marriage and devoted much of the interview to sharing his intense feelings and emotions around how that loss had impacted him personally and professionally.

Ben was extremely articulate during the interview, but so overwhelmed with emotion around his wife's passing that I couldn't help but wonder how a personal loss of such magnitude can totally engulf our senses. We began the interview with him describing his leadership style as collaborative and benevolent. As I asked him about his philosophy of leading, he quickly alluded to how he sees leadership and followership as embedded in each other like two sides of a coin. He felt that leaders must have a dual perspective, and while followers are dancing on the floor, the leader must be present on the dance floor and the balcony at the same time. The psychodynamic construct of the "observing ego" comes to mind. In lay terms, it is a capacity to be on stage and watch oneself from the audience at the same time.

Throughout the interview, Ben made lavish use of metaphors to express difficult concepts. Some of those metaphors are listed in the narrative that follows. Our conversation was lively and colorful, yet there was a ring of sadness as Ben talked about his late wife. The emotional courage that it took to hold that kind of loss was palpable and I wondered how Ben even agreed to be interviewed, knowing fully well that it would dredge up some very painful affect. So how does a leader deal with that kind of uncertainty and ambiguity in one's personal life and make sense of it in other contexts and settings? This was a powerfully emerging theme that came out in the interview.

Emergent themes: Leadership and followership, holding the tension (paradox), intermingling of personal and professional life

Leadership and followership

P: "Embedded within the idea of a leader, is ummm...is followership. So, you know the first time when someone asks me the question how I see myself as a leader, the term leader…my mind always goes to follower, so I always ask my myself the question, how do I see myself as a follower? A leader has to be able to not solve all the problems for the group, but bear them and give them back to the group in small enough, bite size pieces so they can digest it. Using a food metaphor, nutrients that will sustain the group in a direction are also eliminated as waste. This is my better leadership self as described by me."

R: I observed a strong sense of idealization…the "ideal leader" that Ben strives to be.

P: "I can be a soothsayer at times and a royal pain in the ass at other times. I ask many questions of them."

Holding the tension (paradox)

P: "I willingly embrace the recognition somewhere along the line that I have enough knowledge and experience to be valued and successful. I also have the tools available to me to draw upon as I lead others. I feel confident to lead a particular assignment. You know…at exactly the same moment, I feel the burden of the assignment. So in one moment you are gratified that you have been asked to do the work….and ummm…there is a certain amount of praise and flattery, but the at the same time I can see myself on occasion….there is the mud pit in front of me that I have to walk through. Can I walk through the pit without getting too much mud on me."

R: The "mud pit" was a metaphor that may represent the challenges and roadblocks ahead, but also some fear and anxiety that are inherent in work. Ben claimed to masterfully negotiate the paradox.

R: When asked what it meant to be in a paradoxical state of mind, Ben commented: "It's like scotch, an acquired taste…you know, sometimes I wonder what I have done so badly in life to deserve all this, but is …umm….not necessarily schizophrenic… a dual personality takes over…you have to keep your feet in both camps…light and heavy…oxymoronic…small but large. Powerful but weak."

R: Once again, polarity management came to mind as Ben discussed his predicaments with a noticeable air of confidence. He appeared to be a leader who seemed in control without feeling the pressure of polarization. Polarities may be opposed, but can also share a unity of opposition between them. The choice to hold either polarity is not always clear and therefore the only choice available is to hold the two sides together, despite the inherent incompatibility or complementarity.

Intermingling of personal and professional life

R: I asked Ben to tell me about a time when he found it very hard to determine (make sense of) certain experiences. He responded: "You know,…. ummmm…it is actually a non-business example. My wife died 19 months ago and her illness was a long and protracted illness over 4 years, last 12 mos. of which were the worst. Her relationship with her family while always strong internally…ummmm…was filled with missteps and missed opportunities in the 35 years that we were married. It was always a source of great frustration that this…ummmm…. benevolent and tight knit family had a lot of difficulty letting anyone in from the outside. Within the 5 of them there were strong boundaries…walls…her approaching death..many of her aunts and uncles and cousins…friends wanted to be with her for some period of time. Her family, they had descended on the hospice facility, especially last 3 years of her life. But as her husband, I became a sort of gatekeeper for who was allowed in her room and how long. It was a difficult experience."

R: The number of pauses followed by "ummmms" as Ben struggled to make sense of the experience led me to believe that the interview may have stirred up difficult feelings in Ben. I interpreted that as his overwhelming feelings of loss triggered by the recall of painful memories of his wife's death.

P: "I was locked into this experience of death…an experience that I ummm…life threatening disease like cancer…you are suddenly part of a club that you never wanted to join. You fall into a world of cancer, dealing with disease and your own sense of impending loss. It is the single greatest time in my life when I had to lead."

R: Ben's grief was palpable, but it was also interesting to note how he made sense of the enormous pain and uncertainty that had been involuntarily thrust upon him. How he dealt with that ambiguity and made connections with leadership is a point to be noted. The intermingling of his personal and professional life was an important theme that emerged in the interview. I questioned myself. Was the leader's pressing need to talk about his personal life, an outcome of the safety that he experienced in the interviews or was it perhaps out of an overwhelming need to decompress?

P: "First of all, I think that no one…ummmm..truly can compartmentalize their personal and professional lives. It may be the noble lie we tell each other…that what happened at home can be separate from work…it's like saying what happened in our childhood would never influence our lives…that is a grand illusion. Everything affects everything else."

Case 3: Christine (business organization)

Christine is the HR director with a reputable consulting firm. I found her to be highly articulate and open during the interview. She viewed herself as a collaborative and democratic leader based on her personal and professional contributions to her family and friends. The word "democratic" came up several times during the interview, as did "challenge." From her account, she seemed to have experienced a great deal of uncertainty and turmoil in her career, and it was interesting to observe how she made sense of the phenomenon.

This interview was particularly important on certain levels. It was the first interview that I conducted with a leader from a business organization and so I was open to understanding how the experience of working for an employer may or may not be different for a leader, insofar as making sense of uncertainty and conflict in the workplace. The interview was also important because Christine was the only non-Caucasian participant in the study.

Emergent themes: Social justice, workplace bullying, coping and self-preservation, managing and negotiating conflict

Social justice

R: When I asked Christine to tell me about an experience that she found particularly hard to determine in the workplace, she commented:
"Ummmm….ummmm…I think there was a time specifically focused on my career where I would end up working with an organization…with a particular group in the organization that I found very challenging at a number of levels, both personal and professional basis because I found that I was unfairly challenged and unfairly targeted for things that…I think because people were not sure of who they were or their capabilities. And ummmm..they were projecting their issues on me. I was sure of my own capabilities and was confident, but what was perplexing was that the behavior was directed at me from

people above me…. challenging because how can you push back to people who are managing you…how do you defend yourself without offending them? They are controlling your career direction. Do you remain passive and blend in or do you take your frustration out in other ways? It was very challenging. You always have a decision and also a way out. You must use your 'self' to make a change, so I removed myself from that situation."

R: I observed a strong commitment to personal values and the sense of justice that were foremost on her mind. Being unfairly challenged and targeted in the workplace cannot be comfortable for anyone, let alone a person of color. It was interesting to see the intermingling of her personal and professional life. She seemed to manage the anxiety of helplessness by taking charge or by using her 'self' to make a change, as she decided to leave the organization rather than further subject herself to what she perceived to be unfair treatment from superiors. The "dispersing into action" is noteworthy and contrary to the state of negative capability that calls for staying with the uncertainties and anxiety in the face of pressure. Leaders who are unable to contain their anxiety often look for ways to make sense of the situation. The feelings of helplessness can become so overwhelmingly acute that they would rather exit the organization than look for ways to manage and negotiate their challenges, especially if the issues are with their superiors.

Workplace bullying

R: I probed Christine to tell me why she found the previous experience so challenging that she decided to leave the organization. How did she make sense of that experience? She responded: "It's interesting…there is a terminology today called 'workplace bullying.' I did not understand the full definition back then. It was not a subject that was openly discussed. It was my survival instinct. You either stay knowing that it will strip you of your confidence…compromise your values so it becomes a mode of self-survival…survival of self…because it is interesting to read about people who live through horrific abuse from someone close to them and you wonder how they come out on the other side. You have to survive at some level. You don't allow the situation to control you. You don't let your armor be stripped. I absolutely did not want to compromise!"

R: Christine repeats the words survival, being stripped, bullying, and self as powerful indicators of primal instincts and impulses when a person feels helpless and cornered. These may be primitive anxieties, many of which are unconscious. Her unwillingness to compromise with the situation points to her strong sense of self and identity, but also her inability as a leader to deal with workplace challenges.

She further added: It was very demeaning for me…very upsetting for me…catastrophic at many levels because I had this ideal about how one should manage a career…how to interact with people…and that was my script…having encountered that, I had to focus on my survival instinct."

Coping and self-preservation

P: "Psychologically for me, it has an effect on me now where it is stored in my box of lessons learned and is empowering because it is good and bad…. good because it empowers me to react and behave in a manner where if I feel as though I am being challenged in that way, I am equipped to deal with it…that is liberating…unlike before I did not understand how to think about and handle those experiences. But what is still a challenge….it can be a curse too in some ways because you put up a wall, so where I may have allowed myself before, I now refuse to allow myself to experience that again. It triggers those memories. They are reminiscent of those experiences. I get into a defense mode. I am no longer open and friendly. I don't become vulnerable."

R: Christine coped with her uncertain and perplexing experiences by becoming highly defensive and careful about not putting herself in those kinds of situations again. A strong sense of identity is a recurring theme in the interview. When employees find themselves in repeated situations and encounters that challenge their self-worth and identity, they may either retaliate or shut down emotionally, resulting in the unconscious formation of "social defenses" as a defense against the anxiety of further persecution. Christine's repeated theme of self-preservation is an indication that she may have already moved into a socially defensive mindset.

Managing and negotiating conflict

R: I asked Christine to reflect on how she managed perplexing situations at work. Did she sit on them patiently or try to resolve them quickly? Her response: "I like to stamp out fires, but for the most part…I do try…really understand what I am working at before I take action, so whether that takes me 2 days…an hour…or 10 minutes…however long it takes, I react pretty quickly. I don't like to sit on things. As director of HR when I talk to those who want to ruminate, I am like…can you get through this a bit faster? Can we resolve it quickly rather than allow it to fester? People sleep over it and the issue loses impact the longer you sit on it. I like to deal with things quickly."

R: The contradiction was notable between the ideal and the real and also between what she perhaps espoused on the one hand and practiced on the other. She seemed to manage her own anxiety around uncertainty by taking action, rather than engaging in reflection.

Case 4: Janet (business organization)

Janet is an American expatriate of Jewish descent currently working as a leader in an American-owned organization based in Indonesia. This case study was complex on many levels. It can be daunting for an American woman of Jewish descent, currently living and working alone in a predominantly male organization based in a Muslim country. When I asked how she saw herself as a leader, she commented that she herself was the context for her leadership within the context of the workplace.

Janet thought of herself as an agent for the company, a co-facilitator with the employer to get things done. To her, the people she worked with in the organization were foremost. When I asked her to reflect on her underlying style and philosophy of leading and how others viewed it, she commented that she never really thought of her own style and did not know what her style truly was. Recently however, one of her direct reports gave her feedback that he had learned a lot from her style. She commented that she spent most of her time trying to develop people rather that checking up on them. She did not think of herself as a micro manager at all. She seemed very pleased with feedback from her direct report whose own style of leading had been, to try to do everything himself without engaging others or holding them accountable. He learned a lot from her style.

Emergent themes: Interpersonal relationships, self and identity struggle, dialectic of the personal and professional, holding the paradox

Interpersonal relationships

R: I asked Janet to comment on how she felt about the impact on her of people who did not necessarily appreciate her leadership and interpersonal style. She responded: "Of course it helps if the styles are in synch. My style is to help them become independent…thinking strategically…I am not down in the weeds with their business. The problem is that when they want something, they are looking to me to make the decision for them. What they are asking for is less accountability for them. If someone wants to be dependent and not take accountability for his or her decisions, then that style feels not good to me…not good for the business…I do not operate well in that space. I try to coach them out of it."

R: From her comments, it seemed clear that Janet did not want to create a dependency group and was struggling with working in a culture where people typically leaned on their leaders for support, rather than seeking autonomy and freedom of action. Her big struggle seemed to be around how she could add value to those who liked to be dependent on her for recognition, acceptance, and psychological validation. She cited an example of one of her star performers who was dependent and she could not understand why he wanted to continue being dependent on her. It was a source of tension for her because she was struggling with how to make a difference to him. Her way of giving recognition was different from what her direct report may have been used to.

Struggling with self and identity

R: I asked Janet whether the quandary that she found herself in at work wasn't perhaps because of a cultural misalignment. She commented: "Both of these guys are Javanese. They are from Java. I can never be Javanese, but I have learned about the people…I think that some of it is exactly what you might be suggesting. The bigger one is how to be an American leader in an Indonesian-run American company? My identity as a leader…. everyone reminds me that I am an expat…my context is Indonesian…so my dilemma is what part of me still applies in this context? When I said I was confused, you must remember that he…the boss before me was Australian…different culture…different gender. His style was very different from mine, so my star performer is struggling from being micro managed earlier to my hands-off style. That may not be sitting well with him. In the Indonesian context…the school system from High School to University…the teaching style is very rote. People are not expected to question a teacher's authority. The whole culture is status conscious…conflict avoidance. I live with that tension between what a good leader does and what they want…I try to figure out what is driving that tension."

Dialectic of the personal and professional

R: I asked Janet to tell me about a time when she found herself highly conflicted. She commented: "I am leading a cultural transformation right now in Indonesia. I am an American expat in charge of cultural transformation in a foreign country. My overarching challenge is am I getting an authentic response or is it appeasement? I am getting a lot of 'yes, it makes sense' and underneath that is a huge tension because some of the incumbents will probably not match for jobs, so a great deal of anxiety is prevalent. On a personal level I am deeply troubled. These are my dear colleagues. I have worked hard to develop relationships. And so I am feeling badly about it. On the professional level, I feel like the organization has been making bad decisions for years and this is the consequence…hurting people's careers and their families. Six months from now people will look at me as wreaking havoc. Five years from now it may be the right thing to do…there is huge tension. I hate to feel responsible for hurting people who are let go. My husband who was with me until recently is repatriating. I will be repatriating in December."

Holding the paradox

P: "The paradox for me means being on the team and not on the team…the paradox of being on a leadership team and still an American expatriate…. an insider and an outsider…an expert in my field and on the other hand someone who cares. You cannot treat people like tires to be replaced. I am in the role of a coach…the paradox of being an internal certified coach…. impersonal and personal…living in my head and living in my heart. I live with this stuff all the time and I can sleep at night because I am trying to be as authentic as possible and yet be a business leader. What gets me through this tension is an honest caring about the outcome."

R: While it appeared that Janet seemed to be handling the paradoxical tension as best as she could, the inner conflict she was feeling around that tension was intense. She

69

was struggling to maintain her identity as an American woman, a person of Jewish descent, a business leader, and also a caring human being in a male dominated Muslim country. Under the circumstances, she was trying her best to both fit in and be effective; to be liked and appreciated, but also to be respected for her own values and faith. It was a difficult tension to negotiate.

P: "Often times, I am the only female in a male business. I try to manage being female in a male culture...the personal paradox for me is I am Jewish in a predominantly Muslim country. I have been coached not to talk about my Jewish descent. So I can't celebrate my Jewish culture for fear. I am female, but I have to be not too female, American but not too American, Jewish but not too Jewish."

Case 5: Elizabeth (business organization)

Elizabeth is a senior leader with 25 years of experience with a global company that manufactures and markets cameras as one of its product lines. She is currently on two boards. She sees herself as a business executive who has built and led internationally diverse teams. She helps people work together in ways that they may not have before and considers her style to be one of challenger, interrogator, focuser, supporter, and motivator, as opposed to a content leader.

Elizabeth led a consumer camera business that was hemorrhaging money and turned it around. Much of our interview was therefore devoted to her experiences as a leader with that company, both in terms of the severe global challenges and uncertainty that she encountered at home in the US and internationally. She firmly believes in the servant leader model.

Emergent themes: Servant leadership, black hole, managing and holding perplexity, practicing negative capability

Servant leadership

R: Elizabeth's response to my question about her philosophy of leading was as follows:

"My belief is in inclusive and accountable teams where people can contribute. I recognize diversity in the broader sense...skills and knowledge and a diverse team has a tremendous competitive edge over one that is homogenous. The names that come to mind of people who have led social movements...Martin Luther King...to me leadership is what Dr. King did in a much bigger way. Get people to see a vision and rise above what they thought was possible. That to me is the magical experience of leadership. My model is servant leader, great man model…it is all about basic leadership."

R: The servant leader model was an important theme in the interview and is featured here in order to understand how leaders who allegedly practice servant leadership make sense of the study phenomenon. It is also interesting to see how different leaders interpret the model.

Black hole

R: I asked Elizabeth to tell me about a time when she found it hard to determine certain experiences at work and what was it about the experience that made it particularly hard? She responded: "I go back to the camera business. We were losing $15 million in revenue each year. It was the most valuable leadership lesson for me. Initially, I made it all about myself…others had failed before me in doing it. One most important lesson for me…two members of my team came to me and said we can do it together Elizabeth! They could see how pained and troubled I was…and it was so freeing to have them respond to me as a person. And see that I was in a black hole and did not know who to find myself a way out of it. I had no experience of this division. Lot of people questioned my choice to take that role. I was in the hospital with my child. I was the only female in the leadership team. I felt that if I fail, it will be all about me. Having others help me figure it out was provided a fresh perspective."

R: There were several things at play here. First, Elizabeth repeatedly used the expression black hole in the interview, possibly to qualify the feeling of panic, uncertainty, and the state of perplexity. She took up the workplace challenge nonetheless, but felt alone and alienated, making it all about herself until other members of the team offered to help her out.

Managing and holding perplexity

R: I inquired with Elizabeth how she handled perplexing situations at work. She responded: "Ummm…I think you put your finger on it. I look at the data and a situation that I know I have no basis for understanding. I try to get data off the web, reach out to others, and read up on it. I would be more able to address the problem in a more immediate way, but if there is complexity that I don't understand, I would seek to get enough information before making a decision. Something that makes me perplexed, I would consult with others. I may not understand everything there is to know, but I will sit with it. I have learned that most decisions are not totally closed. If you make a decision, you must plan for contingencies."

R: Her biggest quandary was when she made the decision to close their manufacturing plant and R&D in the US and move the operations offshore to China. In the wake of her decision, she faced the possibility that many employees would be laid off; however, it was a business decision to make the operations profitable by reducing manufacturing costs. There was a painful dialectic that she faced between her personal and professional conflict.

She added, "You do it in a humane way, a caring way, but must be firm. I was so convinced we were on the right track…. but I also knew that I was affecting thousands of people. I had an individual, a very senior executive threaten me…he was so angry….it was in the hallway leading up to the garage. I can't repeat what he said, but why he disagreed with my decision…I will use nicer language than he did. He said I was screwing up the organization. I would damage the brand, the company. He reported me to the president and CEO and all because he felt so pained about shutting down our US operations and moving it all to Asia. He decided to become very colorful and used intimidating language. It was a lesson in courage."

R: Elizabeth basically stood her ground even in the face of the executive's threats and I can only imagine the courage that it must have taken to stand up to an aggressive executive much senior to her.

Practicing negative capability

R: I asked Elizabeth to tell me about a time when she felt pressured into making a decision but instead chose to sit with and reflect on it before acting. Her response: "The Japanese were infringing on our patents. It had over time amounted to 20 million in damages for infringement. It was being put off. Finally, I wanted a session in the US and wanted the Japanese leaders to come for a meeting so we could jointly decide the course of action. Prior to the negotiation, I had told my colleagues what I wanted to do. We decided to sit in complete silence…a Japanese culture…. and hopefully we may come to an outcome. As we sat in total silence for nearly 6 hours, the 2 Japanese executives wanted to take a break and finally they came back from the break and agreed coz I had learned from the other Japanese companies the importance and significance of silence. The typical American stance of filling the silence was just not working previously,. Only by using silence were we able to get them in the right mindset."

R: One of the important tenets of negative capability is the practice of mindful awareness in silence without the irritable reaching after fact and reason. The strategy seemed to have worked for Elizabeth.

Case 6: Fiona (academia)

Fiona is a developmental psychologist who currently works as program director at a leading university in the Baltimore area. She has been in higher education since 2001 and is looking forward to moving into a Dean's job. She specializes in the area of adult education, ageing, gerontology, and works with older adults who are 55 plus. She sees herself as a thought leader at the current institution and is involved with curriculum development, getting faculty together, and evaluating and formulating future direction. Her philosophy of leading is one that facilitates the growth of others, providing vision, and sees her style as collaborative. She helps the organization remove barriers. Fiona has been practicing Yoga and Buddhism for many years and finds them to be excellent tools that keep her centered and composed in the face of anxiety and pressures. Emergent themes: Institutional politics, Yoga and meditation, managing and holding the paradox, Buddhism and uncertainty

Institutional politics

R: I asked Fiona to share with me an experience when she found it particularly hard to determine certain situations at work, she reflected: "I can narrate. I have an experience from last spring when I was there as director. There were problems with a person...students were complaining that she was missing in action in the online classroom. It was my responsibility to fix it, but I knew that if I intervened, I would be canned! There was an ongoing relationship between her and the Dean, so I resisted. Unethical issues....so what I did was...I was in a quandary...between a rock and a hard place...what I did was I called a colleague who is tenured. She was fully aware of this graduate assistant and she also knew I could not go to the Dean. So she taught me not to say or do anything right now. She had connections higher up. So it paved the way for me to go to the vice provost and ask for her direction. It was all very frightening and scary for me… did not know what to do…rock and hard place…I could lose my job if I did nothing and if I did say something, I could still lose my job. I am damned if I do and damned if I don't. I was very angry and scared. I was put in a very awkward situation. I was overwhelmed and perplexed!"

R: What seemed most striking here was the politics that Fiona was caught up in. There was a dialectical tension that she was holding between resigned helplessness and action, and yet trying to resolve the issues at the same time. So she sought the help of someone higher up who she could trust. Sometimes, leaders cannot seek others out. They must hold the tension and look for a resolution on their own. This can become an excruciating difficult situation."

Yoga and meditation

P: "When I am feeling anxiety, I do yoga, body scan, meditate…vent to a close friend…and yet at times I cannot do anything. When I get anxious I tend to get into a problem-solving mode. Under the anxiety, there are other emotions…. fear of failure…insecurity…fear of abandonment. Earlier transferences. When I problem solve, it is a way for me to deal with a situation. I need input. It is a feeling of control…. that I am doing something about it actively so I just have to sit with it…hold my feelings. Problem solving is a way to alleviate the anxiety, but also sit back and not do anything about it. If my anxiety is high, there may be something else triggering it."

Managing and holding the paradox

P: "On an emotional level, I can feel anger, hurt, love, different perspectives, all of which can be equally balanced. There is not one right answer for a situation. There is lot of ambiguity. On my MBTI, I am an INFP. When I feel tension at work, I tend to talk about it with my trusted colleagues to get their perspectives so that I may understand it better…that is very helpful. Once I have a better handle on it, I tend to problem solve."

R: While Fiona suggested that she could sit with ambiguity without doing anything about it, I thought that her repeated use of the expression "problem solving" was a way out of the anxiety that arose when she was called upon to hold the tension between two polarities. In my mind, problem solving would be a means of dispersal…. an action of a different kind.

I asked her to comment on "negative capability" if she could.

P: "Negative capability…. very hard to do. I have been meditating for 20 years and yet; I am still working at it to this day. I am looking for a new job and I am sure that if I get a new job, I will have a fair amount of anxiety and meditate with it. Yoga. My internal wine skin needs to be stretched."

Buddhism and uncertainty

P: "I was raised Catholic but I am now a Buddhist. I am stretching through holding whatever is difficult and anxiety producing. Buddhism has helped me hold uncertainty and anxiety."

Case 7: Gordon (academia)

Gordon has spent his entire career in academia. For the past few years, he is the Vice Provost of a reputable institution. Servant leadership was a recurrent theme throughout our interview. He felt that leadership to him meant developing the skills and capacities of other people. It was less about his own competence. He was not seeking personal glory and believed in removing the barriers of others while creating a shared vision of where they were going and what they were achieving. He is not a highly directive leader and instead, tends to be more supportive.

The interview with Gordon was extremely illuminating and shed light on "negative capability" from the perspective of a senior academic leader who suddenly found himself caught in a very challenging situation at work. His direct boss who was the Provost, and his direct report were allegedly colluding against him. He was under enormous tension.

Emergent themes: Philosophy of leading, interpersonal conflict, dialectical tension, Buddhism and uncertainty

Philosophy of leading

P: "My focus is on people development. Maximizing their potential…give them an opportunity to try and fail as well as try and succeed. My peers and directs reports see me as follows: One camp sees value and they value that. I am not highly directive. I am supportive. I try to be a coach to them. There are others that don't like it because they are struggling with their own development. They look more for traditional leaders who say that you are great and wonderful."

Interpersonal conflict

R: I asked Gordon to reflect on what it meant to him to have some people at work who were not happy with his leadership. I probed him on this issue in order to understand how his style may or may not have been be affecting his ability to live with the uncertainty of his situation. He responded: "I am wrestling with that very issue right now. The first level is to find a space in servant leadership. How can I communicate with this person, meet their needs? The other aspect is that there are some people that the challenge with them is that there is no common ground…generally what I do…like a parent with my kids…letting people have an opportunity to fail…to not be critical…just let them be…what went right, what went wrong? How can we learn from it? I have a direct report; she is Director of the doctoral program, who has a direct relationship with my boss the Provost. So I can't coach or challenge my direct report and address her development and coz she is being mentored by my boss, she feels she is smarter than me…and so it becomes very frustrating. How can we reconstruct the relationship coz this is not going to work anymore?"

R: Gordon's comment was very revealing. He was finding himself in a serious quandary. There was a part of him that would have liked to support the direct report, but he seemed highly conflicted and struggled with how to hold the dialectical tension. So in the end, he felt that there might not be a way out of the situation. This was a difficult impasse. How do you reprimand your direct report if she is colluding with your boss against you?

R: I further probed Gordon on this situation in order to understand how he made sense of it. His commented: "So I had a difficult meeting with my boss yesterday…it takes two to tango. One thing is a follower who skips a level and continuously does that. Maybe has a personal relationship with a level up or a mentoring kind of relationship, but when it becomes a manager a level up; she also has bad habits and my boss is empowering her behavior. My boss does not check things with me first and instead sent a message to my direct report's peers inquiring the status of something."

Managing dialectical tension

P: "The struggle is what are the actions that we can take? In this situation it is about trying to determine the actions I have available to constructively engage in the situation. I have told my close colleagues that I am in a no-win situation. If something goes right, my direct report will take credit. If it goes wrong, they will both make me the scapegoat. There is nothing I can do to break that impasse. In computers we call it the 'deadly embrace.' My direct report right now…coz I am a scapegoat, it will be blamed on me. So if we remove the scapegoat…she is not as astute as I am. My boss will turn on her. My boss is very abusive. I think she has been in an abusive relationship growing up and so she equates negative and critical…as this is how you are going to grow."

R: I found this comment and the metaphorical reference to the "deadly embrace" interesting. In computers, a deadly embrace is a situation in which two or more competing programs or actions are each waiting for the other to finish, and as a result, neither one ever does. Gordon was in a serious predicament as he sat anxiously with knowing and not knowing. This was an intense period of uncertainty for him. He took the support of some trusted peers, but also knew that he would have to ultimately deal with it alone. The triangulation and dynamics of three (the boss, Gordon, and the direct report) was a difficult impasse. He considered himself to be a scapegoat (victim) and there was a ring of fatality that probably emerged from a state of helplessness and panic.

Buddhism and uncertainty

R: At one point in the interview I asked Gordon how he was managing his anxiety and work and if he had truly removed his stake from the outcome. He replied: "Yes, I am trying to do that. The metaphor that comes to mind is from Frank Herbert's Dune books. …A key ritual that occurs is the idea of taking something poisonous and converting it to something useful. Once you finish your doctorate, you can read fiction again…(LOL)…You can take poison and metabolize it into something else. And at an intellectual level, I am trying to say that there is poison…toxicity in the work setting…you can succumb to the toxins…you can remove yourself from the environment…all the depression, anger, frustration, stress, and anxiety or you can accept the toxins and convert them. Or the other story that I have gained a lot of strength from is Buddhist enlightenment. Meditating under the Bodhi tree. That idea is not in the western modality, our tradition is…if something that is done to us is violent, we win by being stronger in our response. Someone brings a knife to a fight and we bring a gun. It is all about escalation. The eastern perspective embraces the uncertainty and negativity and converts it to something beautiful and harmless."

R: Gordon's use of metaphors was very revealing. He was trying to make sense of his quandary and at different times in the interview he vacillated between anger/frustration/helpless and a place of calm introspection where he was trying to make sense of his situation. He made several references to the Buddhist notion of mindful awareness during our conversation. The dysfunctional mentality so prevalent in the workplace seemed to be a source of great distress to him. Words such as fighting, guns, knives, bigger guns, and escalation, all pointed to a crescendo that made Gordon very uncomfortable. That is not who he was at the core. He was struggling with how to hold his sense of values/servant leadership philosophy with earning a livelihood and taking care of his family.

Case 8: Harry (academia)

Harry is a Fielding alumnus who entered academia several years ago after running an OD consulting practice for nearly 25 years. He cites his love of teaching as his primary reason for the switch in careers. His wife has been very supportive. As a leader in academia, he sees his role as mentoring students. He feels that he has some power and authority over students, which is very different from private practice. One of the reasons that I recruited Harry for the study is because I thought that he would be able to provide a dual perspective, both from the standpoints of private consulting and academia.

As it turned out, Harry had some very rich and unique experiences to share with me. He discussed some deeply disturbing emotions around the uncertainty that he feels in his current position and how he is trying hard to hold and manage the tension. Despite some painful experiences, I did not find Harry to be reticent about his affairs.

Emergent themes: Career shift, mentoring, making sense of difficult experiences,

Shifting careers

R: I asked Harry how he saw himself as a leader. He responded: "Well, it has changed. I made a later career shift when I got my PhD. I am now into academia for the past few years. I told my wife I'd love to teach. It's funny, when I was a consultant and met my second wife; I was consulting with a BA degree. She said you are too smart to be using others' deliverables. She saw a theoretical bent in me that I had not seen in myself. She encouraged me to pursue higher education. In academia, my thirst for theory is satisfied.. I enjoy mentoring as my style of leading."

R: A drastic career shift from private practice into academia is not something I have seen too often. People transitioning from private practice typically tend to take up consulting jobs with companies. How this shift to academia was impacting Harry and perhaps contributing to his predicament was most interesting.

Mentoring

R: "Mentoring" came up often in the interview. I asked Harry to reflect on what mentoring meant to him. He commented: "The role models for me are my professors at Fielding. They are not lecturing us. They are not telling us what to do. They are simply drawing out from us. I am helping adults learn and grow in their careers. Mentoring is quite fulfilling, but the part that is not pleasurable in academia is when I have to grade students. I don't like to do that, but it comes with the territory. I have a mantra from a philosopher…Robert S. Hartman. He suggests 4 steps…know yourself, choose yourself, grow yourself, and give yourself to a cause bigger than yourself. I believe that there is no better experience than to help students in higher education…not just accept themselves, but also choose. Lots of people try to give of themselves before they know themselves or develop themselves."

Making sense of difficult experiences

R: I asked Harry to talk about a particularly difficult experience at work that he found hard to make sense of. He replied: "One I am going through right now; the other when I was at the dissertation phase at Fielding that you are at now Anil. I uprooted my family. Moved from California to Salt Lake City. My wife agreed that I could go on a nationwide search in academia. You know that Fielding is not very well known in academia. They look at our model as totally online like University of Phoenix or DeVry.

It is extremely competitive in academia. It was frustrating to spend 150K at Fielding and have people not pay close attention to a Fielding degree, but for me personally, it was a phenomenal experience. People with degrees from Harvard, UMC etc. have a huge edge. They are seen as great research universities. My transformational coach asked me to hold that tension. You cannot resolve it, so that is a space you must stay in. and that advice served me well. My wife and I have lived apart for 18 mos. in order for me to hold this job. I uprooted my life, bought a new home here in Salt Lake and now my uncertainty is around the fact that I am coming up for renewal and don't know how that will go. For me, my tension around this uncertainty is going through stages. Last spring, I was very uptight...my uptightness was not well received in the classroom...you lose awareness when you are caught up in your own stuff. Then I said to myself, I cannot control what others say about me. I will do the best I can. I am good at my work. If that is not good enough, damn you! I'll go somewhere else! For me this has gone through stages. First stage was stress. I had a shingles outbreak last summer, probably related to this. Then in shifted to anger...how dare they do this to me...a phase of being mad...and then I really...this coach who helped me before said to me..let go of the outcome...so now I say to myself. 'I have taught my best these past 2 years...if they think I am not good, I cannot control the outcome.' I am better for it. But I think I'll probably renew for the next term."

R: The various phases Harry went through in order to contain and manage his anxiety around the uncertain situation could have an enormous impact on a leader's ability to be present with all his senses. How can you be emotionally present and be yourself when your mind is experiencing the possible threat of losing a job? Later in the interview Harry shared with me that he goes through a similar pattern when he is perplexed...stress followed by anger, followed by resignation and acceptance. At one point I asked Harry if for some reason he lost his teaching job, would he consider returning to private practice? He flat out said no. He would just go and try for another academic position.

Case 9: Ian (private practice)

Ian is in private practice as an OD consultant and works predominantly with healthcare companies. While he has previously worked for employers, he has been on his own for the last 5 years. His greatest strength is to see patterns quickly and to help his clients understand these patterns, so they can decide what to do with that information. He does not necessarily need a title to lead and believes that a formal title is not necessary in order to practice good leadership. He cites the example of Ronald Reagan as a charismatic leader. Whether you agreed with his politics or not, he got people to rally around his leadership.

Emergent themes: Leadership style, holding and managing uncertainty, paradoxical thinking, managing and holding polarities

Leadership style

P: "By and large, I was one who was much into helping others learn. I was interested in creating a learning environment. I was primarily a coach to my direct reports…my assumption was that good people would do a great job. I wanted to get out of their way, but if they became stuck, I would help them get out of their stuckness. I had people who had higher needs for structure than I was able to provide. Thus they felt frustrated. I was reluctant to provide too much structure. That was probably one area that I could have done better at with addressing their needs."

R: During the interview, Ian spent a lot of time talking about how he was able to quickly identify patterns in interpersonal situations, almost to the point that he was accurate most of the time. It was a strong theme for him. He prided himself in his ability to coach and mentor his people and help them with their developmental needs.

Holding and managing uncertainty

P: "The way I handle perturbing experiences in the workplace is that I find people to vent to. I also maintain a sense of humor…what I have found is that there is BS everywhere…One of the nice things about getting older is that even though I am frustrated, I can say to myself…'this is another blip…this too will pass. I will do the best I can.' It is not about disengaging, but staying centered and composed. I can demonstrate that I can be productive rather than dredging up past issues. When faced with uncertainty, my preference is to resolve it. Sometimes, it is simply a transaction with certain people. This is a terrible metaphor…I have gone in to negotiate to buy cars and the car dealer acts as my friend…they are not my friends…. they just want to close the deal. A recruiter for a company is like a car salesman. They close the deal and move on."

R: It was interesting how Ian seemed to manage uncertainty at work. A point worth noting was that he maintained a sense of humor even in difficult situations.

Paradoxical thinking

R: I asked Ian to talk about what he understood by paradoxical thinking in light of his experiences. He commented, "About 20 years ago, a dear friend of mine was facilitating a training program where she was talking in the context of a tool she was teaching. She said that she goes, in essence, from one paradox to another the whole day. At one level it is paradoxical and then levels of abstraction…most people want to do their best, but people get stuck in their own issues…for me what is helpful to connect with the higher level of things. Once I see a higher level need in a situation, I can work with it. Until then, I am in a quandary…no resolution. We have to find a frame where we could meet both our needs."

R: Ian was able to hold the paradox on the one hand, but rather than staying in that paradox, he moved it to a different level of abstraction. So was he perhaps seeking a way out of his dilemma or was the reframing simply a way of staying where he was, but only rethinking the situation differently?

He added: "The thing about paradox is, it's a maze. There are twists and turns…imagine looking down like a general at the battlefield. When you are in it, you cannot see clearly. But when you pull yourself one level, you can see it clearly even though you are still in a paradox."

Managing and holding polarities

R: I asked Ian what strategy he would deploy if he found himself party to a conflict where there was a growing impasse with the other party? His response: "Many times you can resolve the issues, but must first get acceptance to engage in dialogue. There is a difference between telling someone that you are in a bind and that you need his or her help vs. confronting someone. You are seeking the help of someone. I can start with my own tension that I feel. A bind…let's go from there. I feel a tension in my body and I use it as a motivator to have this conversation with the person, but in the long term, this incident becomes a template against future actions."

R: In this situation Ian used his self, his feelings, and his physiology to approach a conflictual situation in order to resolve it. He was genuinely seeking the help of the other, which can be a helpful strategy.

Case 10: Janice (academia)

Janice is a trained media psychologist who currently works as an adjunct faculty member with an academic institution. She sees herself as someone who inspires collaboration and makes sure all voices are heard. She considers herself to be a quiet and gentle leader. Sometimes that can be a bit challenging because she finds it hard to be forthright. Her leadership philosophy is collaborative.

Emergent themes: Interpersonal conflict, making sense of perturbing experiences, discomfort with silence

Interpersonal conflict

P: "I recently experienced a huge conflict with a fellow colleague and there was a lot going on that did not have to do with us directly. There was a lot going on, but when we had the time and space to talk about it, I did not confront her…that is not the way it is, but I did not back down either…we were just able to explain…we are not disagreeing with each other. We just had different approaches. It was an approach to a student and how we can allow them to learn. I was okay with them making a mistake and guiding them…a lot of that came in that direction. I hate using the word mistake…we are always dealing with someone's perception…my approach is, I might think that something is right or wrong…I am always dealing with their reality. What is my goal? Is it to feel better about myself? My goal is to not feel vindicated, but to get something done…to move forward with someone."

R: Janice used negative capability to help resolve the conflict. She recognized that different people have different approaches. They have different realities.

Making sense of perturbing experiences

R: I asked Janice to tell me about a time when she found it particularly hard to determine certain experiences. She said: "Easy! When someone is silent, not necessarily in groups, but also face-to-face interaction…so let me pull it out when I don't understand the other person. When I understand, I am fine, but I don't I feel frustrated. That is the hardest. So I take it deeper…in an interpersonal situation when someone is

83

silent and non-expressive. I know something is not right, but I don't know what it is. I straddle both an introvert and extrovert. But I am basically an introvert. I need to push myself to get out there extrovertly. It does not come to me naturally. Because I come from a place of wanting to understand someone's experience, if I can understand what they are thinking or what their issues are, I can then make some decisions on how to approach them…but with no feedback I just feel like I am throwing darts at the board and hoping that one hits the bull's eye! Hit or miss. I don't deal well with hit or miss. I am organized and structured. I don't deal well with chaos. I look for certainty."

R: It is useful to note that in one scenario, Janice was perfectly content sitting with and not doing anything to resolve the conflict with her peer, perhaps because she knew what was happening. There was certitude. But on the other hand, when someone was silent and she did not know why, she felt frustrated and sought out certainty rather than sitting with the person's silence in an attempt to understand it.

Discomfort with silence

R: I further probed Janice on her challenge with silence. She responded: "And that is what I was saying. You asked what's the most challenging and difficult for me when I am facing someone's silence. In essence, I lose my power of leadership at that point coz the way I am good at leading is to draw my strength by being able to understand someone else's situation. I hate the idea of control and I gain a lot from what someone else has to say. I hate to say that I control it, but in a way I am controlling it. This is an area of learning and growth for me. I am completely in agreement that if I keep prodding them…keep at them who are silent, I am only agitating that situation. They just might need that time and space and it is not helpful for me to project my discomfort on to them."

Case 11: Kelley (private practice)

Kelly made a transition into private practice after a successful career with one of the big four accounting firms where she was a senior leader. She holds a doctorate in depth psychology and currently owns a practice in executive coaching and Jungian analysis. Her specialty is working with corporate executives who are dealing with a great deal of conflict and strife in the workplace. She also teaches part-time.

I recruited Kelly for the study because she brings a unique perspective, both from the standpoint of corporate life and psychotherapy, in addition to her involvement in academia. She shared her experiences with a great deal of candor, especially those that I thought contributed significantly to understanding the essence of "negative capability."

Emergent themes: Servant leadership, working at the edge of uncertainty, corporate politics, paradoxical thinking

Servant leadership

R: I asked Kelley how she saw herself as a leader. She responded: "I am a leader in my field. …Ummmm…How do I see myself? Boy, I have always had strong feelings about leadership in corporate. I lean to the servant leadership model. In depth psychology, the way that I express myself; lots of researching on myself in how I express and conduct myself and then using my self,. I teach also."

Working at the edge of uncertainty

P: "I feel….ummmm…that the edge of not knowing is critical. If I find myself in the knowing…ummmm…then I know that in some way, I am attached to something that may not be true…and I am always throwing my ideas out to be reworked. There is humility. It's so weird…what I want to say is that there is certainty in my uncertainty. To feels certain, to me feels wrong. I will give you an example. In my career now, I am so in my moment…a client of mine has a major crisis…I completely rely on my intuition. I say that 2 personalities will generate something new…so I feel in my past career with XYZ Company, if I did not know what to say, I kept quiet. Now I am more able to openly express myself. If you are coming in with knowing, then you are already filtering the person with your own beliefs. You are only seeing with your own projections.. I want the moment to be alive…to not filter the experiences through my projections. The relationship is with the ideal, not the person. That is how it is with certain relationships. People cling to the ideal and miss the person emotionally. Not that people are confused. They just make the ideal real! You cannot penetrate the idealizing transference with a client until trust and safety are present."

R: I observed a strong theme here of how Kelley successfully used her self in order to understand the other. Her thoughts around uncertainty and not knowing were poignant.

"Idealizing transference" is a psychotherapeutic concept, and in therapy, this transference must be penetrated in order to emotionally reach a client. It is not an easy process of engagement, for the client will unconsciously put up a wall of resistance when a therapist creates that transference.

R: I further probed Kelley to tell me about a time when she found it particularly hard to determine certain experiences at work. She responded: " I have a couple that I am working with now. I am not a psychologist who works with disease. I am more of a counselor. So when a person approaches me with a mental health issue, I am totally confused. When I am in the unknown, I am thinking now about this very damaged couple…most of the time it is how to say what needs to be said and hopefully it will land somewhere, but in this last session, things were really difficult. It was almost as though they both turned on me. Ummmm…but I really had no idea how to get out of that situation. I wanted them to leave my office. I wanted the session to be over. I wanted to give them to someone else. They are borderlines. It's a very difficult situation in therapy. They are also unconsciously manipulative. I was overpowered. Their unconscious is strong…you are at their mercy…they will control your unconscious. I knew that was happening. I was having an emotional reaction. Normally I do not show any emotional reaction, but my projections are always there. This time though I showed a reaction. I knew that I was rendered powerless by her unconscious. I knew that was happening and I could do nothing about it so I shut down. I knew there was nothing I could say or do. I just wanted to keep them out of jail. …Keep them from calling the police on each other."

R: This was an emotionally charged, highly volatile and virulent situation shared by Kelley. Therapists are trained to practice negative capability, and yet, in the heat of the moment, everything can suddenly become unbearable. This is an example of how challenging it is for someone to be in the negative capability mindset for any length of time.

R: In response to my further prompt, Kelley added, "there are two places I was jarred! The first was when the man got angry coz I did not fix their relationship. I am mirroring a relationship behavior. What the right response for me was. His girl friend was not able to do that…I was jarred! You know, they thought they were paying me to fix their relationship. It is far more complicated than that. I was feeling angry and misunderstood. So my reaction was…I don't need that from my clients! But I also wanted to show them how to have a conversation with each other. In that same 2-hour session, later on, the woman who rarely shows me her borderline, she just stood up in the last 45 minutes and screamed at me!!!!! I shut down!! There was nothing I could do. This never happens to me because I typically put a shell around me…it was a bad session!"

R: Kelley was in a situation where she felt very scared and anxious because in her mental state, she could neither make sense of the experience nor know how to maintain her own composure. It was interesting how she repeated the words "jarred" and "shut down" twice. We often encounter painful situations such as this that feel like a deadly embrace; a conundrum that we just cannot get out of. We can neither contain, nor process it in that moment! Our patience is tested to its very limit.

Dealing with corporate politics

R: I asked Kelley to try and recollect and narrate some of her past experiences with uncertainty in corporate. She commented: "Yeah, in corporate, I did not sit with it very well. Most of my career I was doing projects. I was managing multiple projects. The corporate environment did not lend itself to sitting on things. In my last job, if I had to sit on something, I had to close my door and not have other seeing me sitting…doing nothing…reflecting. I am an INTP, which means that I have to have introverted thinking time to give my best answer. My last boss was an extrovert. I told him if you keep talking, I couldn't't give you the answer. He once came into my office and sealed his lips. He said he was being quiet…LOL. In the corporate setting, the only time they ever get to see me..They (my clients) think that my office is a sanctuary. It is a SPA for the mind…they get to sit and reflect…Not at home, not at work. I basically see corporate executives as a therapist. I see the problems…the same that I saw when I was in corporate."

P: "In 1999, I took a month off to visit Australia and New Zealand. When I came back…I had been a senior manager for many years…they took one of my clients and they gave that account to a new senior manager…MALE!! Lot of male/female shit going on…I asked, am I chopped liver? There is a lot of haughtiness…I noticed some male managers…they would talk at clients! I came back from overseas and had no work! I had to start from scratch! This sort of gender gap…in my soul I said…am I going to fight it or am I going to…and that is when I started to realize that I would not last in corporate for too long!"

R: Kelley's comments were intriguing. The struggle she experienced as she tried to survive against all odds in the workplace and the enormous pressure of losing one of her most valued clients to a new manager while she was away on vacation overseas was painful. And she finally reached a point of despair and decided to leave the corporate setting. Gender came up a few times in our interview and she thought that the corporate setting was a man's world even today. She'd rather be in charge of her own destiny than subject herself to emotional abuse in the corporate setting.

Paradoxical thinking

R: Kelley's thoughts on paradox from a Jungian perspective were interesting. She commented: "This is the theme of Jungian psychology. Jung is very clear on holding the tension of opposites. Life is all about paradox. It is always relative. When you are absolute, you are lost. Transcendent function…dialectical tension…that is where Jung is going from an individuation perspective…Unhinge the ego. Bring in the spiritual side. Bring the ego and soul in a dialectical relationship. People seem most perplexed about relationships…one of the ultimate existential issues is I vs. We. We are all connected. But I am also an I. How do you navigate losing the eye and being in relationship?"

Case 12: Lori (private practice)

Lori is a private consultant who specializes in communication coaching. She leads by action, as she makes use of a body and mind holistic connection. In some ways, she does not see it as leadership, but rather in terms of relating to people. In her mind, if that means giving difficult feedback, she prefers to deliver it in a kind and directive manner. She mostly finds herself facilitating others' work. Her clients see her as attentive, warm, and gentle. She is told that she asks really good questions.

Lori's participation in the study proved to be particularly useful because earlier in life she had worked with the controversial Werner Erhard, the founder of the EST Training and later, the Forum. Erhard was essentially self-taught and yet rose to prominence as a leading thinker in personal transformation. Some regard his now defunct organization to be cultish. After he retired in the 1990's, he sold his practice to his followers who went on to form the Landmark Forum.

This interview has also been an example of how personal loss, as in the sudden death of a beloved friend can throw one's world into a state of turmoil and disarray. Lori loses a dear friend to cancer and how she deals with those difficult feelings is very moving. How one makes sense of those emotions contributes in some way to understanding a person's phenomenological worldview. Ironically, events such as this can be dramatically transformative.

Emergent themes: Holding and managing difficult experiences, loss of control
Holding and managing difficult experiences

R: I asked Lori to share an experience from the past, which she found to be particularly troubling to hold and think about. Her commented: "Hmmm…what comes to mind early in my work life... I worked for Werner Erhard and managed one of his centers in the 70's, and there was a lot going on that I would say I had trouble making sense of. It mostly had to do with the gap between what I saw being done and how people… those in leadership above me…how they spoke and behaved, versus what was being taught to others. I was young…in my mid 20's and it was a time where in my center, with the way I was running it, we were hitting all our numbers and my the staff was happy, yet there was a lot of negativity toward me about how I was doing it. I was being kind, and gentle, and supportive, and that wasn't the usual way. I think what really made it hard for me to make sense of… I really believed in what we were doing…I was passionate about it…naïve…and so I think that one of the things that made it hard was I could not reconcile the fact…that…what's the word Argyris uses? Theories in use and theories in action! I was very idealistic. I believed in what was being taught. But the closer I got to Werner himself, it became extremely confusing. Up until one particular phone call with him, a long call… it was definitely troublesome. At the time, I handled the confusion by …ummm….thinking about it all the time, ranting about it, fighting about it…talking to my direct supervisor until she really didn't want to talk to me anymore. I really went after it. I would be more reflective today. I would talk with my husband, and listen to his feedback. I would ask myself questions like what am I feeling? Why is this getting to me? What's really going on here? Big picture? I am much more self-reflective now!"

R: Lori's account was an example of how we can feel manipulated in the workplace, especially if we are inexperienced. Her idealization/ambivalence around Werner was quite evident. I know that many people who worked for him felt manipulated at the time. And despite that, they would continue to hero worship him. Many people felt damaged in those experiential workshops led by Landmark Forum. It was a control tactic; how to control your mind in order to achieve your goals in life, except that the methodology and framework used were very coercive and high handed. For a young person like Lori to have to face that quandary must have been a painful experience. Lori handled the confusion and perplexity by talking and fighting over it. At one point she shared with me in the interview that the only way that her boss Werner Erhard would listen, is if you yelled at him!

She added: "In the past, as I said, I felt very righteous…holy righteousness, and I rallied to save it from killing itself…But with that energy, with that pain that comes with thinking a big bad thing is about to happen, I took on the job of trying to save it.. kind of holy righteousness."

Loss of control (unconscious)

R: I asked Lori to talk about a situation when she was called upon to summon all her competence in order to hold the tensionality. She comments: "If I bring it down to micro moments. Think of something overt. I was sitting with clients several months ago. It was a couple. I work with personal communication…it is relationship and communication coaching…not full life coaching. I was listening to them and going…I have no idea what is going on. Oh my God, what have I got myself into? The tension, misunderstanding, and blaming were all a mess. I'd been working with her and this was the first time she was with her fiancée…and that's an example of .. "I don't know what's going on!" I sat there listening; I genuinely did not know what to do. Did not know how to help them. I was very engaged, but also feeling reactions in me to what was happening in front of me….the tension between them…watching their body language…I can see the pattern unfolding. I am aware that in that moment, I did not know what to do. At other times I sit with clients and don't know what to do but it does not matter because I know I will soon. The answers will soon emerge, so there's no tension there. At other times I am going; what the…(you can fill in the blank!) am I doing here? Typically I have a sense sureness in a situation, but the one that was a not knowing, the one harder to hold the tension in…it was because they (the couple) had a lot of negative emotions flying…their emotions were very intense. I was probably feeling their stuff… they are beyond cranky, resentful, and those are neurobiological energies that don't stay contained within them. A heightened level of emotions in clients isn't unusual, but it is harder when there are two people with me… the dynamic of three... It was really their emotions that were difficult."

Case 13: Mary (business organization)

Mary is the OD manager for a large engineering company. In her hybrid role, she spans boundaries across several regions and businesses. Her leadership style is inclusive and nonhierarchical. The matrix structure of the organization is congruent with her style. She expresses a deep passion for psychodynamics. One of the challenges that the company has recently faced is in the area of inclusiveness and diversity, so this interview was particularly relevant to the topic of the study, given similar challenges being faced by other large organizations.

Emergent themes: Servant leadership, challenges with diversity, holding and managing perplexity, psychodynamics and unconscious
Practicing servant leadership

P: "When I think of myself as a leader, I am as a partner, a servant leader, working together to help people feel important and included. Not telling them what to do. Let's get there together. I see myself not as a genius, but a genius maker. I tap into the collective intelligence of the group. It is important to me to know that in service to teams and individuals, I like to be included and part of the team and also have others be a part of the team. I see excited when I see the light go off in their eyes and they discover something without me providing any answers. Also, the light goes off in my eyes when I learn. It is a mutual learning exchange and relationships based on trust. It is all about trust. Another element is huge. Diversity. I do a lot of diversity work here. I learn from and appreciate differences."

Facing challenges with diversity

R: I asked Mary to comment on a past experience, which she found to be particularly hard to determine. She responded: "Yeah, I have two. One was a great experience and one was frustrating. I think about it a lot. It has to do with…as we are in a very innovative business environment here…we have a theory Y organizational structure….a unique corporate structure to have people experience the work culture well. I was in a situation a while ago when some of our associates were not feeling valued and heard. We had a higher than normal turnover. On the surface, it made sense that these folks were not able to stay employed with us, but it did not make sense to us, we dived into it and found that they were not receiving accurate, timely, and heartfelt feedback. When they did receive it, it was too late. Now 6 years later we have a low turnover and our minority feedback score is high."

R: I probed Mary to find out what was really going on. What was it about the minorities? Were people afraid of giving feedback to minorities?

Mary responded: "People had a fear that if we give a minority person honest feedback, they may take it as discriminatory! There is a whole unconscious perception about the angry black male…we had to break through that…we had to let the minorities know that if you were not part of a meeting, it is not because you are black…there was an internalized depression among the minorities. Also, the side giving the feedback…By the way, I will stay anonymous, right?"

R: I assured Mary that this was totally confidential. I wanted to dig a bit deeper into this dynamic so I let Mary talk more about it.

P: "The unconscious bias for blacks and other minorities is significant! The core issue we identified was with blacks for the most part…honestly we have not seen it other ethnicities. Our data points to a lot of improvement at present. We do not want any division and separation that may cause chaos now."

Holding and managing perplexity

R: I asked Mary how she handled perplexing situations when she was faced with them at work. She replied: "I sit with it for a while and then I like to get a group of influencers; people who were affected by the change. I am big on getting the whole system in the room…appreciative inquiry…what needs to change? What is working? Rather than get mired down in a problem solving approach."

R: When people are able to talk about their experiences, it may mean that they are transforming. When they can rise above the angst and frustration and be able to talk objectively without their physiology getting magnified, changes begin to occur, so getting the whole system in the room and teasing out the issues seemed to have been a good strategy for Mary. Notice that in Mary's account, she was not trying to "problem solve," as several other interviewees said they would have done. Instead, Mary engaged the whole system. In a sense, she perhaps found it hard to hold the uncertainty and so tried to seek others out to process it.

Psychodynamics and unconscious

R: Mary shared with me during the interview about her interest in psychodynamics. Given that we share a common interest, I asked her to talk about it and how she deployed it in order to make sense of difficult experiences in the workplace. She responded: "I do look at things through a very psychotherapeutic lens. I do not accept that someone with issues wants to be a poor performer. We all want to do well. I am very pleased over the years that by listening to people, you can identify people who need therapeutic and counseling help. Once their interpersonal issues are resolved, their performance improves. I love the psychoanalytic perspective in groups and teams…. things are mostly psychological."

R: I asked Mary to narrate a past experience when she felt particularly anxious and conflicted at work. She commented: "One comes to mind instantly. It was before I took the OD role. Or perhaps just was getting involved…before I started therapy…. I had a mentor in my company who had helped me a lot. She opened a lot of new pathways for me. But when I went to graduate school, she felt very upset! She felt abandoned by me. My mother died when I was 21, so she was almost like a mother to me, also a mother when I went through a divorce. When I decided to attend grad school, she was really upset. She felt abandoned. In her mind she felt that I needed her less. I was reeling from rejection as well. Because she was a mother to me, I could not be objective about her. There was a transference and countertransference. She was happy as long as our relationship was parent-child, but not when it changed. I wanted

93

equity; she wanted power, albeit unconsciously. I felt very rejected. I felt as though I lost my Mom all over again! I felt very sad coz I had lost a workplace mentor…it was okay professionally because by then I had a lot of credibility. Today because of my work in therapy, we all have unconscious biases that are being revealed to us, but is less likely to happen now. 9 years of therapy has helped me a lot!"

Case 14: Norman (academia)

Norman is an ex-marine who has been working in academia for the past 15 years. He had been feeling very disgruntled lately on account of some unexpected episodes at work. The dialectical tension that he felt between his allegiance to the students and the commitment to the institution was an important theme for him. Much of the interview dwelt on the tension surrounding this uncertainty. How he manages and negotiates this tension sheds some important light on the study phenomenon.

It is important to note here that Norman had entered a doctoral program in OD at Fielding, but decided to withdraw, in part because of the disillusionment that he feels with academia at the present time.

Emergent themes: Servant leadership, holding and managing perplexing experiences

Servant leadership

R: When I asked Norman to reflect on how he saw himself as a leader, he responded: "I have always looked at the classroom as sacred ground. There is trust involved with the students and institution. I am much more into students! That feeds into my leadership model. I have a responsibility to students. I take that job very seriously. I like to think of myself as a servant leader. But there is a problem with that jargon! It is overused. My job is to take the curves out of the roads so it can be smooth sailing for students. I am not a boss in the classroom. They are my customers. In addition to teaching, I am also into program development and intake advising. My style is both facilitative and servant leader. Leading from behind is a good descriptor!"

R: The tension that Norman felt in his role began to leak out in this very first comment. It was an important cue and I probed it further in the interview in order to understand it better. I suspect that this tension is experienced by other academics as well who feel

94

conflicted between serving the students well and surviving in the politics of an academic institution.

Holding and managing perplexing experiences

R: I asked Norman to share with me a particularly disturbing experience at work that he found hard to make sense of. He responded: "The thing that jumps out to me..I already alluded to…it was to do with the Masters program. The satellite program, which was housed in the community college. We teach upper division adult learners. The MBA program got left off. Students had been asking for it. We started it up. I started recruiting students. I had 27 students apply. They even took their GMATs. Even though the institution was in dire financial straits, we found out later that we could not do it. The main campus hemmed and hawed…delayed and then flat out said we cannot do it this year! The Dean said 'your little program is not going to impact us favorably.' So, how do I wrap my mind around that? I still can't! They were screaming for funds…there were all the right reasons to do it…and yet they dumped it. I was very perplexed, very angry. Based on their commitment, I made commitments to my students. I was very excited! And then I felt betrayed!!!! I felt a huge amount of betrayal! They have me take the initiative, do the work, and then pull the carpet out from under me. This cavalier attitude was very infuriating to me..The betrayal of trust!!! The authority. Ultimately betrayal of taxpayers! Lots of negative emotions. I took it personally! Right now as I talk to you, I am getting all choked up here!!!! I had to do the dirty work. I crafted a letter and got it cleared by the campus. It was very sparse…matter of fact. I had students call me, but could not talk about it. I was told by the college not to engage the students. Students were very reticent about my lack of responsiveness. They formed a community…beating the drum. Telling their story…all that came down on me…the main campus came down hard on me…the students were all disgruntled taxpayers. My job was not to quell them. It was all projected on me!"

R: This was an interesting development and very telling from the standpoint of the dialectical tension he felt between serving the students and dealing with the institution. Betrayal was a word that came up several times during the interview and I wonder what the ramifications of feeling betrayed can be on a person's psyche. Here was a high-energy idealist who wanted to get things done, but was getting caught up in the

95

quagmire of politics at work. As an ex-marine, he was probably an assertive individual who believed in social justice and fairness. He couldn't help but take the betrayal and disappointment personally. A loss of perspective and deep sadness are attendant feelings that are often evoked in the wake of such a betrayal. That said, someone else in Norman's place who could potentially play the politics, may not have felt as fazed. Institutions often demand from their employees a sense of resilience in the face of difficult situations; however, not every employee is able to manage those expectations.

R: Norman became suddenly reflective after sharing the emotionally charged episode and added: "I have probably gotten into trouble by being too forward…should have sat on things more. I do stop and think, but my stance is to be inclined to action than inaction. I kind of resonate with…it is better to beg forgiveness than ask permission. I am not a loose cannon! I do follow rules, but I do push issues. I have never knowingly violated a policy. Or undermine authority…but my allegiance is to students!! I asked Norman to tell me how he felt about all the issues. He commented: "I am very angry, arrogant…gosh, well there is a saying in the Marine Corps. 'I have already been to boot camp!' If I look back there is noting you can do that will get to me…you are welcome to try. But it is kind of an arrogant response on my part. It is not going to affect me. That was not a good place to be…arrogance is not a good trait…nor is feeling superior. Now I know why I don't like phenomenology…. LOL!!!!"

R: The process that Norman went through in the interview of making sense of his feelings was informative. From contradicting himself to questioning his actions led me to think that the entire episode had left him in a state of confusion and disarray. It was not easy to recount difficult experiences. He second-guessed himself several times during the interview.

Holding a paradox between serving students and serving the employer

R: I asked Norman to share with me what he understood by paradox in light of his specific experiences at work. He replied: "You know I have been very negative about my institution, but I would like to mention though that I have a duty to my students, but I also have a duty to my institution…their standards and guidelines. I take a paycheck from them, so I am willfully disobeying….well Anil, help me here…this is how I see it. I have a responsibility to both. I think that I actually served both sides well…an institution is not just the people who make the decisions....their leaders...they are making decisions that are totally wrong...if it came out into the public, it would seriously damage the institution. I don't know...I feel that I was doing the right thing, and yet, on some level, I was disobeying the institution."

R: Again, Norman vacillated between what he did and what he should have done. At some level he was questioning whether his previous actions had served him well in his career. On the other hand, he felt the pull of allegiance to his students and what he construed to be the right course of action.

Group Analysis:

Having completed the individual analyses for the 14 case studies, I now turn to analyzing data for the entire group. This will be completed in 4 steps:

1. Listing of the recurring emergent themes as they appear in individual cases, including key phrases and metaphors (Box 1.1 following the appendices). This is a partial list (raw data) that may not include some items that appear in Box 1.2. The list includes all random keywords and expressions that become the base from which the group-level themes were extracted.

2. Clustering of themes (Box 1.2). Similar themes from Box 1.1 may appear under one or more clusters because they share similarities or highlight differences. The process of identifying and developing superordinate themes includes abstraction, subsumption, polarization, contextualization, numeration, and function (Smith et al, 2009, pp. 96-98)

3. Master listing of superordinate themes (Box 1.3)

4. Group narrative

Box 1.2 (Clustering of Group Level Themes)

1. Difficulty with making sense of self and identity (how one constructs and makes sense of self and identity in social settings)
Feelings of helplessness
Self-preservation
Unfairly challenged/targeted at work
Demeaning behavior
Workplace bullying

Social justice

Liberating

Triggering old memories

Values and tolerance

Being stripped of one's confidence

Core respect

Sense of validation

Guards go up/red flag goes up

Career shift

Double-guessing

2. Intermingling of personal and professional life (the impact of what is happening in one's personal life and its bearing on our professional life and relationships)

Loss of spouse

Loss of beloved friend

Locked into the experience of death

Hospice care

Gatekeeper for dying spouse

Holding loss for the other

Breaking down

Shingles outbreak last summer because of work stress

Making sense of loss

Insomnia

Not the brightest candle in church

Dying

Know yourself, choose yourself, grow yourself, give yourself to a higher cause

Like scotch: an acquired taste

Cancer: You are suddenly part of a club you never wanted to join

Losing my mentor felt like I had lost my mother all over again

It may be a noble lie we tell each other that what happens at home can be separated from work

Moved family from the east coast all the way to Salt Lake City

3. Mentoring and coaching (how our interpersonal style and philosophy at work help shape our relationships and interactions)

Diamond in the rough

Pygmalion effect

Kegan's work on consciousness and evolving self

Framing and reframing

Levels of consciousness

Levels of abstraction

One foot on the gas, the other on the brake

Action vs. reflection

Kegan: Socialized mind, self-authoring mind, self-transformative mind

Unlike the Buddhists' comfort with uncertainty, I want to know and have an impact

Mentoring is fulfilling. It is a pleasure

Robert S. Hartman's model: Know yourself, choose yourself, grow yourself, and give yourself to a cause bigger than yourself

4. Buddhism and uncertainty (understanding and deploying the important tenets of Buddhism as they relate to comfort with doubt and silence)

Comfort with discomfort

Non violence

Meditation

Removing stake from outcome

Mindful awareness

Embracing doubt

Comfort with not knowing

Control is an illusion

Buddhists' comfort with uncertainty

Going to pieces without falling apart

Thoughts without a thinker

5. Dealing with corporate politics (**the social, psychological, and emotional impact of workplace politics on one's well being and capacity to be productive at work**)

Betrayal at the hands of boss

Triangulation between self, boss, and direct report

Collusion between boss and direct report

Scapegoating

Workplace bullying

Manipulation

Unfair targeting

Projecting bad feelings on another

Irrational behavior

Lack of clear-cut objectives

Feelings of incompetence

Double-guessing oneself

Loss of control

Boss will not let the issue go. Even though the situation is not on fire anymore, it is still fresh in the boss's mind

If something goes right, my direct report will take credit. If it goes wrong, she and my boss will scapegoat me

Persecutory anxiety

No objective measures stated in my performance appraisal to say that I meet the goals

Anytime I make the measures objective, my boss shoots it down

Toxic environment

My direct report gets giddy as a school girl when she receives special attention form my boss

6. Discomfort with managing and holding polarities and paradox (understanding that polarities and paradox are a part of everyday life, and learning to hold them, as opposed to dispersing into action may be a productive skill)

Problem solving

Feeling the impulsive need for action and dispersal

Pregnant pause

Discomfort with ambiguity and not knowing

Comfort with discomfort

Fear of looking stupid, fear of losing relationships, fear of not progressing

The need to know drives behavior and action

Deadly embrace

Impasse

Deadlock

Difficult bind

Need to know, need to understand, need to resolve the issue

Self-doubt. Is a lie still a lie if you don't realize that it is a lie?

Even though I know there is a problem that needs to be addressed, I may not act out of fear

7. Important lessons from personal loss and adversity (how a personal loss can not only immerse oneself in grief, but also transform the way we look at life and relationships)

Personal situation with mental health issues of sons makes me the coach I am today

During my wife's death, it was the single greatest time when I had to lead

I don't allow myself to experience those painful emotions at work anymore

Not going to tolerate certain behaviors anymore

Created an armor around me

When direct reports fall into dependency and want to be micro-managed, the red flag goes up for me. I coach them out of dependency

8. Exercising servant leadership (understanding that servant leadership is more than being attentive and collaborative to the emotional and psychological needs of those that we work with. It may also imply becoming a container for the anxieties and uncertainty at work)

I let people struggle and maybe even fail. I don't fix things for them

Compassionate leadership, empathic leadership

Democratic style of leading

My behaviors demonstrate my leadership

Collaborative effort that empowers people

I am a co-facilitator with my company to get the job done

We work as partners

Help people become independent

I do not operate well in a space where dependency is being created

Respect culture and gender differences

My ultimate goal is not to change my style of leading to adapt to others

I believe in vision and inspiration, but also accountability and measurement

See myself as a thought leader in adult learning

Provide vision and a collaborative style

Mentor to students

Some power and authority over students

Mentoring is fulfilling. It is a pleasure

I am very feminine in my leadership. I am always about power with and not power over people

There is a haughtiness in some male managers

9. Managing and negotiating uncertainty and conflict at work (recognizing that conflict is not always unproductive and uncertainty not always a call to action)

Have lived away from wife and family for the past 18 mos. just to be in academia

Great fear of losing my job if my contract is not renewed

In academia I have to sell myself every 3 years in order to be renewed

Go through a process of enormous stress, anger, and release. It is also transformative for me

On the far side of the paradox, lies a resolution. To hold that tension is the way to respond. You cannot force a resolution

Stress may get temporarily alleviated, but the tension remains

I find myself licking my wounds many times over

When someone is silent, I try to pull the person out of that silence

10. Framing and reframing perplexing situations

Looking at problems differently

Higher level of abstraction

General looking at battlefield

Seeing new patterns

Tackle issue you most want to avoid

New cognitive lens

Not avoiding confrontation
Seeking resolution

Box 1.3: Master listing of group-level superordinate themes

1. Exercising servant leadership
2. Intermingling of personal and professional life
3. Discomfort with managing and holding polarities and paradox
4. Difficulty with constructing a sense of self and identity
5. Dealing with corporate politics
6. Adverse experiences of managing and negotiating uncertainty and conflict
7. Challenging experiences from personal loss and adversity
8. Framing and reframing perplexing situations
9. Buddhism and uncertainty

Group narrative

Several superordinate themes are listed in Box 1.3, chapter 4. Some of the more salient recurring group themes are discussed here in the order of importance and frequency with which they emerged in the interviews. In the interest of reducing redundancy, I have chosen not to repeat the leaders' verbatim accounts unless I think that they contribute to strengthening a certain theme or otherwise illuminating convergence and divergence. The reader is directed to the previous section where detailed accounts were included with individual cases.

Exercising servant leadership:

More than half of the study participants referred to themselves as servant leaders. They passionately described their leadership style and philosophy to be collaborative, democratic, empathic, and compassionate; however, the manner in which they dealt with uncertainty and conflict at work seemed to be at odds with how a servant leader might manage the challenge. This was a puzzling dichotomy. Is it possible that leaders hide their true feelings and emotions at work, so that their peers and direct reports are only able to see a side of them that they want to show? Would that be consistent with servant leadership? One of the tenets of servant leadership is vulnerability; therefore I wonder what impact if any such suppression may have on a leader's psyche.

Servant leadership is not a new philosophy. It goes back to Lao Tzu (2006) in China and Chanakya in India who both wrote about and practiced the art in ancient times. In more contemporary times, Greenleaf (2008) coined the expression in 1970 in his essay "The Servant as Leader" and it has come to be associated with a model of leadership that is somewhat idealistic. The expression is now used loosely even though it continues to enjoy a high status in the leadership lexicon. Servant leaders believe in sharing power and place the needs of others before their own. Such an individual is not at the top of the pyramid, as is often the case with an autocratic leader.

When asked how their peers and direct reports saw them, the leaders' accounts were consistent with the manner in which they thought others viewed them. The leaders that I interviewed had no previous ties with me personally or professionally, therefore I think that there may have been an unconscious need to be seen in the interview as astute and benevolent. I experienced that my opening question put the participants at great ease, which may have contributed to the safety that they felt to talk about some deeply disturbing issues later in the interview.

I observed a connection between "exercising servant leadership" and "practicing negative capability." One of the hallmarks of negative capability is "annulment of the self" in order to understand and immerse oneself in the other. Keats addressed the notion of a "chameleon poet" as someone who is forever changing and adapting in order to open oneself to life's richest experiences. One cannot practice servant leadership without becoming a servant to the people that one leads. Like negative capability, servant leadership too may be an ideal to strive for, but difficult to achieve. Intermingling of personal and professional life:

Participants for the study were purposively recruited because I thought that they would contribute something of value to an understanding of negative capability from a professional standpoint. When I asked them to tell me about a time that they found it particularly difficult to determine (make sense of) certain experiences, and what it was about those experiences that made it particularly difficult, many of the participants recounted personal rather than professional experiences. In the true spirit of phenomenological inquiry, I did not interrupt or otherwise shortchange the conversation at that point because I believe that what emerges naturally is data in its purest form. I could sense that their energy was vested in past events of a personal nature that seemed to have an important bearing on the way that they made sense of the phenomenon at work. Once I was able to harness their energy, it was easier for me to steer them back to talking about professional matters. By then, some very rich data emerged from their personal accounts.

In case 1, Amanda shared with me her terrifying experience of having to live and deal with two of her grown sons who are suffering from mental health issues of a serious nature. One of her sons suffers from chronic OCD and the other from chronic anxiety. In case 2, when I asked Benjamin to reflect on that question, he narrated to me the extremely painful experience of losing his wife of 35 years to cancer and what he went through while she was in hospice care. As we were discussing his feelings and emotions around that episode and how it impacted him, he commented: "No one can compartmentalize their personal and professional lives. It may be the noble lie we tell each other that what happens at home can be separated from work. It's a grand illusion. Everything affects everything else."

Janet's (case 4) struggle with not being able to celebrate her Jewish culture, religious beliefs, and gender as an American expatriate living in Indonesia; Lori's (case 12) loss of a very dear personal friend, Mary (case 13) losing a mother (mentor) all over again, are examples of how personal experiences juxtapose and intermingle with our professional lives. And yet, there is very little patience or space within contemporary organizations for leaders to express their deepest fears and anxieties in a safe setting. This suppression may over time, contribute to the formation of "social defenses" (Menzies, 1960; Czander, 1993).

Menzies writes: "If social defenses are forced on the employee they perpetuate pathological anxiety…These defenses are oriented to the violent, terrifying situations of infancy, and rely heavily on violent splitting which precipitates the anxiety" (Czander, 1993, p. 112)

Is it easier for leaders to deal with and discuss uncertainty in their personal lives rather than their professional lives? Is the open outpouring and articulation of personal episodes, perhaps a defense against the anxiety of thinking and talking about their professional issues? This has been one of the most important superordinate themes that has emerged in the study and warrants further research. While we discussed professional episodes of a sensitive nature as a result of my probes during the interviews, the workplace issues were not foremost on the minds of many participants. I wonder why that was the case. Had I insisted that the leaders talk only about professional issues, I would not have access to this important data from their personal life experiences.

Negative capability is about being comfortable with ambiguity. It calls for staying in a liminal space. Benjamin (case 2) suggested that our personal and professional lives are difficult to compartmentalize. He called it the grand illusion. I suggest, that in the interviews, narrating past experiences inevitably meant that several leaders had to come to terms with their deeply disturbing personal issues as well. For some, these pressing issues were perhaps percolating for sometime. IPA is a methodology that emphasizes the importance of affect and feelings. Given its origins in health psychology and the kind of studies that have been historically conducted using the approach, it is also sensitive to understanding participants' deeply disturbing issues of a personal nature.

As I attempt to make sense of this important group superordinate theme, I speculate that participants perhaps found my empathic and compassionate interviewing style to be comforting. I may have become a safe container for their personal narratives. If they had the capacity to hold both their personal and professional sides without feeling polarized, it is possible that they would not have felt the need to share sensitive issues of a personal nature with a total stranger like myself.

Discomfort with managing and holding polarities and paradox

At the time of recruitment, all the leaders were apprised of the study topic. In a series of communications, they read and understood the meaning of the construct before agreeing to participate in the study. When asked to reflect on how they managed to hold difficult paradoxes and polarities, the participants commented that they made sense of the experience by engaging in the following actions and behaviors as represented in figure 2.1 below.

Figure 2.1 (Schematic representation of holding polarities and paradox)

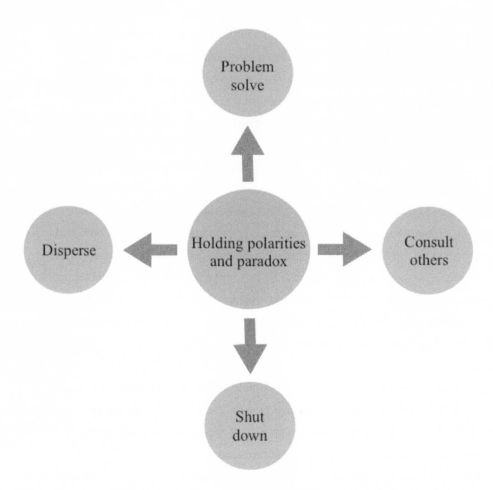

In the interviews, leaders commented that they typically adopted one of 4 stances when faced with paradoxical dilemmas which they found challenging to hold:

- Get into a problem-solving mode in order to understand the situation.
- Reach out and consult confidants at work who may shed light on the situation.

- Emotionally shut down in the face of an impasse where no clear resolution is in sight.
- Disperse into action, which may include engaging in a string of explanations or rationalization. It may also include inviting the other party to a conversation in order to break the impasse or bind. If the anxiety becomes too intolerable, the leader may decide to exit the organization.

It was evident that leaders found themselves to be highly conflicted in challenging situations that called upon them to hold polarities and paradox. Chapter 2 included the work of several theorists such as French, Elson, Batchelor, and Baxter & Montgomery who have contributed to a greater understanding of this complex dynamic. From the standpoint of the study, it was important to understand how leaders made sense of the contradiction or complementarity inherent in paradox while resisting the pressure of polarization. In the literature review, I have discussed in detail how these notions are informed by "relational dialectics" and "dialogism." The pull of polarization often occurs when our capacity to stay with doubt is diminished. Batchelor (1990) suggests that doubt is neither a "cognitive hinge, nor a psychological defect, but a state of existential perplexity. It is not resolved through adopting a set of beliefs and achieving a pseudo-certainty" (Batchelor, 1990, p. 16).

While the leaders' accounts were largely anecdotal and derived from personal experiences, doubt and uncertainty seemed to be pervasive. We construct our own realities, and because phenomenological inquiry does not set out to prove, disprove, or refute hypotheses, the only way to enter someone's life world is through their retrospective experiences of a personal and professional nature. The emotionally charged nature of the conversations lent a great deal of credence and reliability to the individual accounts, notwithstanding some contradictions that were also present. Where possible, I probed further in order to understand the meaning of those contradictions. Leaders seemed to manage the dialectical tension in a number of disparate ways.

In chapter 1, I discussed a leadership 360 Degree Feedback Model (figure 1.1). I had suggested that leaders who are able to practice negative capability, exhibit certain behavioral skills such as authenticity, comfort with ignorance, patience, reserving judgment, tolerance for ambiguity, exercising servant leadership, empathy, and awareness of situation dynamics. Many of those skills seemed to imply that leaders be comfortable holding polarities and paradox. The study suggests that in highly uncertain and perplexing situations, leaders' capacity to contain the paradox is diminished and they engage in behaviors that seem to alleviate the discomfort of uncertainty. This finding will be more carefully examined as I develop future applications for negative capability.

Difficulty with constructing a sense of self and identity

In highly uncertain and perplexing situations at work, leaders seem to struggle with making sense of their identity and self worth. Christine (case 3) articulated with a lot of passion how she had been unfairly targeted and challenged at work by her superiors and the helplessness that she felt at the time, knowing that there was nothing she could do about it. As the only leader of an African American background in the study, I wonder if her race and gender had anything to do with the issues that she struggled with. She described in the interview, the demeaning behavior of her supervisors, the feelings of being stripped of her self-confidence and self-worth, and the erosion of trust, all of which seemed to have contributed to the unconscious development of a highly sharpened survival instinct.

Janet's account (case 4) was also telling from the standpoint of self and identity. She struggled with her own feelings as she described in the interview that as an American expatriate of Jewish origin working in Indonesia, she was unable to be herself in the workplace. She worked for a male-dominated company in a Muslim country and was never quite sure if the natives considered her to be a part of their team. She was unable to celebrate her Jewish culture openly, had to downplay the fact that she was a woman, and even though the company was American owned, she realized that she would never be accepted as a Javanese. The dialectical tension that Janet was experiencing at work could not have been easy to hold.

In other accounts shared by leaders, Elizabeth and Kelley (cases 5 and 11) narrated how their gender became a serious handicap at work, despite their level of competence. Elizabeth was viciously assaulted and threatened in the parking lot, albeit verbally by a very senior leader in the organization because he thought that she was "screwing with the organization" by leading an initiative to move their American R&D

operations to China. She was the only woman on the team heading a global initiative, and it was likely that she was targeted for that reason. Many men are not very comfortable with women in senior leadership positions and the fact that Elizabeth was a strong and talented woman, perhaps made the senior executive very uncomfortable. Her predicament around holding the dialectical tension between doing what was right and human by the employees whose lives she was likely impacting, and doing what was right for the company was not easy. She knew that her actions would impact the livelihood of hundreds of dislocated employees.

I see important linkages between this dialectic and the theoretical constructs posited by Baxter and Montgomery (1996). Commenting on the dialectics of connectedness and separateness, the authors suggest that these improvisational inner dialogues are at the heart of communication.

Kelly shared a disturbing story of how her company leaders (mostly men) took one of her most important clients and gave the account to a new manager while she was travelling overseas on vacation. Upon her return, she had no work and had to rebuild and rise, literally from the ashes, which was not easy to do. While she could have fought and defended her rights, as many men in the company would have done in her situation, she chose instead to not react. She struggled with feelings of being treated like a second-class citizen, possibly because she was a woman. At that point, her mind was made up that she would not survive in a male dominated corporate culture, and so decided to leave shortly thereafter and go on her own as a Jungian therapist.

The women leaders described here all seem to have been stigmatized. Goffman (1963) describes "social stigma" as emanating from the perception of race, identity, gender, physical appearance, sexual orientation, religion, and ideology. While these stereotypes are not openly discussed in the workplace, they are unconsciously mobilized and impact interpersonal communication at "levels of abstraction" that are out of our conscious awareness.

Elson (2010) draws our attention to these "levels" as they relate to various paradoxes in a wide range of contexts. Understanding these unconscious processes means recognizing that a paradox may be unresolvable. You can only bring it to conscious awareness if you lift yourself up a level. Even though you are embedded in a new paradox, the situation becomes clearer. Ian (case 7) made an interesting analogy of a general looking down upon his battlefield. As long as he is embedded in battle, he is unable to see the field clearly, but when he lifts himself up, it all starts to become clearer. Goffman (1963) "frame analysis" would also be an example of looking at the same situations through different lenses. Wilden (1972) writes, "no communication can be properly defined at the level at which the communication occurs…This sentence is in English" (Wilden, 1972, pp. 113; 172).

In working with negative capability since 2002, it has been my experience that women may have a greater struggle with making sense of their identities in the workplace. Men tend to externalize their feelings, while many women hold their feelings inside. While a man may choose to openly discuss his issues with a boss, a woman who is feeling a loss of identity, may instead leave the organization rather than deal with a demeaning situation. This is not to suggest that there are no exceptions. It may or may not be coincidental that in cases 3, 4, and 11, Christine, Janet, and Kelley decided to leave the workplace rather than deal with a compromised sense of self and identity. Had they practiced negative capability, they may have chosen a different course.

Dealing with corporate politics

Throughout the interviews, there were several glaring examples of politics in the workplace, which seem to have seriously impacted the leaders and thrown them into a state of mental disarray and perplexity. Ironically, these examples are mostly within the context of academia, and in all three cases, the academic leaders chose to leave their institutions, as opposed to dealing with anxiety in other ways. I would refer to their exit as a classic form of "dispersal" (French, 2000) when the anxiety becomes too intolerable and difficult to contain and must therefore be defended against by removing oneself from a toxic and persecutory environment.

While politics is virtually endemic and unavoidable in contemporary organizations, it is interesting how the leaders managed and made sense of their internal and external strife. What were the feelings that got evoked as a result of the conflict? Were those feelings internalized or externalized? What were the psychological ramifications of holding that anxiety and how might such virulent anxiety adversely impact our physiology and emotional well being, not to mention our personal relationships? We can never know for sure, based on the data alone, however, the leaders' accounts do provide a pattern of similarities and convergences that seem to suggest the virulent impact of politics in the workplace.

Gordon (case 7) was Vice Provost of an academic institution where he had been employed for the past 2 years. His current boss who was Provost did not recruit him to the institution. She was herself promoted from within. His direct report was the Director of the Doctoral Program and was promoted to that position by Gordon. At the time of the interview Gordon was in a state of great mental anguish and uncertainty. His direct report had of late, started to overstep her authority and was colluding with the Provost. His boss was also harassing him and it was becoming extremely difficult to manage his subordinate.

As I entered Gordon's life world, I could sense his feelings of trepidation, self-doubt, and fear. He had a large family to support and was extremely worried about what might happen if his boss would try to terminate him. The feeling of being scapegoated by his boss and direct report was very overwhelming and the not knowing had started to play havoc with his psyche. Every time he proposed to his boss that she should add "objective" measures for him to strive for in his performance improvement plan, she would disagree with him, and instead, insisted on "subjective" performance expectations. She was also becoming belligerent, emotionally abusive, and highly disrespectful toward him. Gordon had not disclosed to his wife and family until recently that he was having serious issues at work. He decided that he would wait until things got resolved at work. When he did finally share it with this wife, she became upset and wondered how they would take care of their large family. At the time of writing this narrative, I hear that Gordon has already left his current employer and is getting ready to join a smaller institution on the west coast. He may consider leaving academia altogether if things do not work out in the near future.

Fiona (case 6) was Program Director and Curriculum Manager at a large university. She holds a doctorate in developmental psychology and is passionate about working with adults and the senior population. She had been employed at the university for many years and enjoyed her job; however, of late she had started feeling very uncertain and greatly disturbed on account of serious unethical issues that the Dean and a teaching assistant were involved in. They had been colluding for a while and even though their misdemeanors did not impact her personally, she was feeling deeply disturbed and angry. In her own words, she found herself "between a rock and a hard place." She added: "I would lose my job if I did not do anything and still lose my job if I did something." It was an impasse that she was unable to resolve. The way that she managed her inner conflict and quandary was by meditating on it everyday, while trying to find a way out. In the interview, Fiona shared with me that she had "just about had it" and was actively looking for another job, possibly as Dean at another university. Meanwhile, she did seek out the counsel of a trusted colleague at work who advised her to not do anything about the situation at work. I can well imagine how it must have been for Fiona to be in such a difficult impasse.

Another interesting account of an academic who found himself caught in the quagmire of institutional politics was Norman (case 14). He is an ex-marine who had been in academia for the past 15 years. While the individual case 14 in the previous chapter provides a detailed account of his issues, I do want to highlight here how politics at work can shape the manner in which an employee makes sense of uncertainty.

Norman considered his classroom to be sacred ground and perceived himself to be a servant leader working in the service of his students. His allegiance to his students far outweighed any allegiance that he had to the employer. As a hard charging, results oriented individual, he had been feeling deeply disgruntled with politics at work, especially those politics that directly or indirectly impacted the students that he taught and advised. He felt highly polarized and was taking things quite personally. At one point, he even felt personally betrayed by his employer when a decision was made to not go ahead with the MBA program, which he had been entrusted to lead.

I interpreted Norman's issues to be around the balance (dialectic) that he constantly struggled to achieve between being there for the students and being there as a representative of the institution. That balance seemed to tip easily in favor of his students. He was even willing to "fall on his sword" for a just and righteous cause. It seemed hard for Norman to paradoxically hold both sides with diplomacy. I recently learned that Norman was so disgusted with academia that he has decided to leave it altogether and pursue a different career.

Looking at the difficult situations faced by Gordon, Fiona, and Norman, through the lens of negative capability, "dispersal" comes to mind. In all three cases, the leaders found it challenging to stay with doubts and uncertainty without the irritable reaching after fact and reason. They decided that the anxiety was too unbearable and defended against it by exiting the organizations where they were employed.

Adverse experiences of managing and negotiating uncertainty and conflict

While all the strategies discussed here serve to reduce uncertainty and anxiety at some level, they also enable leaders to make sense of the phenomenon. If however we take into consideration the purest definition of negative capability, none of the leaders that I interviewed (with the exception of Kelley who is a trained Jungian analyst), seemed to have a propensity to hold the tensions for any length of time. From their accounts, it was clear that they all sought some form of resolution or action; a way to escape the quandary, as opposed to staying with not knowing and not doing.

Framing and reframing perplexing situations

Several leaders in the study passionately discussed how they made sense of and even discovered new ways of looking at their perplexing situations by using a process of reframing. A "frame" is a cognitive lens, a set of notions that we entertain in order to make sense of the world. "Reframing" is questioning our existing mental models and having the courage to break existing frames (Goffman, 1974; Kegan, 1994). Bolman & Deal (2008) discuss how Home Depot's new CEO Bob Nardelli eventually failed in his new position. They write: "He was a victim of one of the most common afflictions of leaders; seeing an incomplete or distorted picture as a result of overlooking or misinterpreting important signals" (Bolman & Deal, 2008, p. 4). The authors suggest that reframing requires that leaders look at the same situation in multiple ways.

In the study, I observed several leaders rushing in to make sense of uncertainty in ways that they knew best, such as problem solving, shutting down, consulting others, or dispersing into a string of defensive routines like rationalizing, explaining, and acting. These defensive routines are unconsciously mobilized and largely out of awareness. In the face of uncertainty, leaders seem to fill the void with what they know, what they can

114

get done, and how quickly they can resolve organizational issues. The world of leaders is a smorgasbord of confusion, frustration, and uncertainty, therefore it is not altogether surprising that these routines are resorted to as a defense against the anxiety of failing or not looking good in the workplace.

Voller (2014), a psychotherapist in UK suggests that negative capability is an advanced ability that comes with practice. It entails listening intently to what the client may be saying, helping that individual reframe the predicament, and allowing oneself to be perturbed by the client's transference, while staying in the mode of not knowing. By virtue of their training, these professionals create a "therapeutic alliance" with the client, such that both can remain in a state of uncertainty for extended periods of time. It is an excruciatingly painful sense of "unknowingness," almost like a state of "reverie" which is not immediately rewarding, suggests Voller. Existentially speaking, it means coming to terms with "dasein," the essence of being or simply what it means, "to be" (Heidegger, 1999).

I realize that the challenge with holding the negative capability frame of mind may arise from a leader's inability to know what it means to be in that state. It must be internalized intellectually and emotionally, but also demands a lot of practice with holding, containing, and refraining.

CHAPTER FIVE

Discussion, Findings, Experiences, and Implications

The individual and group analyses in the previous chapter illuminate how leaders made sense of uncertainty and conflict in a variety of ways. They typically "dealt" with perplexing situations rather than sitting and reflecting on them patiently. They became "instruments of action" rather than "instruments of thought." As I immersed myself in the research, I discovered that the study was both expansive and eclectic. It was also inconclusive in some ways, and yet, it offers a unique opportunity to look at life, work, and relationships differently. Later in this chapter, I try to construct a definition of negative capability that may be more practical and germane to our postmodern times. It is a way of viewing the phenomenon through my own cognitive lens, while recognizing the limitation that any formulation I offer is only an interpretation, and not the canonical truth.

Batchelor (1990) a Zen Buddhist scholar suggests that there are three factors that need to be cultivated in our quest for new knowledge: great faith, great doubt, and great courage. The "faith to doubt," writes the author, "does not refer to the kind of wavering indecision in which we get stuck, preventing any positive movement. It means to keep alive the perplexity at the heart of our life, to acknowledge that fundamentally we do not know what is going on, to question whatever arises within us" (Batchelor, 1990, pp. 16-17).

Uncertainty and negative capability: A meta-theoretical exploration

There is not one body of knowledge that illuminates the phenomenon in its entirety. Negative Capability is informed by several meta-theoretical discourses in the field of interpersonal communication. The "Relational Dialectics Theory" and "Dialogism and Dialectics" were covered in the literature and are examples of theories that are grounded in the interpretive tradition. Other theoretical constructs are rooted in the post-positivist and critical perspectives. It is beyond the scope of this study to enter a discussion of each paradigmatic framework; however, knowing that other ways of looking at the phenomenon exist, helps to understand it in all its complexity.

116

An unexpected outcome of data analysis was the emergence of extant theories that I had not previously considered. These theories have their origin in the post-positivist tradition and are important from the standpoint of better understanding how individuals make sense of conditions such as uncertainty. Simply recognizing that leaders are uncertain does not tell us how they receive, evaluate, and respond to difficult experiences. It is also important to understand how they process the information and make sense of it emotionally, cognitively, and psychologically. A brief outline of three theories of uncertainty follows:

Problematic Integration Theory (PIT)

Babrow (1992) developed the theory in order to understand the role that uncertainty played in interpersonal communication. It was originally informed by the "post-positivist" paradigm, but later morphed into the "interpretive" framework. Afifi & Matsunaga (2008) posit that if someone is uncertain about a situation, but is certain that a search for information will result in a positive outcome, the uncertainty is reduced and the situation becomes unproblematic. This however, is not very often the case, and so people frequently live with uncertainty and ambiguity for extended periods of time. Babrow believed that if there is agreement between the "probabilistic" (the probability of an expected outcome) and the "evaluative" (its value) orientations, the integration is in harmony. These are socially constructed realities. The problem stems from the conflict that occurs between what one expects and what actually ends up happening, making the integration more difficult.

By way of an example, let's consider the situation of Kelley in case 11 who discovered upon her return from a month long trip overseas that her biggest client had been transferred to a new manager in her absence. She felt dejected and very worried. At one point she even considered approaching her boss for answers, but upon reflection, decided that she would rather stay with the uncertainty than subject herself to the ridicule of her fellow colleagues, most of who were men. Fiona in case 6 learned of a misdemeanor involving her boss and colleague, but was caught in a dialectical tension, knowing that whether she acted or didn't, she would have to face the consequences. She then turned to a senior colleague for assistance, even though she realized that there was no guarantee that the situation would be resolved. As a result of

117

her quandary, she continued to live with the paradox of knowing and not knowing, and over time learned to deal with her chronic anxiety.

Amanda (case 1) was an example of someone who had been struggling with enormous uncertainty and anxiety on account of her two sons' illnesses for many years. She tried very hard to manage the anxiety by getting educated in OCD and mental health; however, over time she realized that there was only so much that she could do to help. She had reached a point of resigned helplessness. Her mental state of knowing and not knowing had morphed into something chronic. She chose not to intervene and further enable the dysfunctional behavior of her sons and decided instead that she must live with the situation without trying to fix it. I would consider Amanda's state of mind to be similar to negative capability, where one stops looking for answers and chooses to stay with doubts and uncertainty. It may be kept in mind that Amanda may not have chosen that disposition of her own volition. It was thrust upon her, given her excruciating circumstances. This is unlike the stance that a trained psychotherapist may take consciously, when opening up negative space with a client.

Uncertainty Management Theory (UMT)

Developed by Brashers (2001a), the theory makes an interesting departure from the commonly held belief that uncertainty always precipitates anxiety. It emphasizes the meaning that people make of uncertainty, our emotional response to such uncertainty, and the psychological strategies that we employ in order to manage the uncertainty. The author also delinks uncertainty from information and suggests that one may have an abundance of information about something, and yet feel quite uncertain about it.

Brashers posits that uncertainty may cause a myriad of other emotions, not just anxiety. He provides an example of how people sometimes manage their uncertainty around difficult situations, such as getting tested for illnesses like STD or HIV, by choosing to not get tested (and know the outcome), rather than deal with the knowledge of something catastrophic or life threatening that a positive test may indicate. Both the avoidance of information and the search for information serve to manage uncertainty. Individuals living with consistently high conditions of uncertainty, often adapt to chronic uncertainty. Giving the example of someone living with HIV, the author suggests that these individuals tend to focus on short-term goals that feel more certain, as opposed to planning for long-term uncertainty (Brashers, 2001a).

Leaders who participated in the study used a variety of cognitive and psychological strategies to manage their uncertainty. Fiona (case 6) resorted to problem solving and Buddhist meditation in order to deal with her difficult situation at work involving the unethical behavior of the Dean. Gordon (case 7) shut down psychologically and chose not to intervene because he feared that his boss, who was colluding with his direct report, might terminate his position as Vice Provost. He made sense of the uncertainty by choosing to reflect on it in silence. He opted not to confront his boss and find out what was going on, out of fear that he might discover an unfavorable outcome. Harry (case 8) described the process that he goes through when dealing with uncertainty. It involves going through the 4 stages of anger, stress, acceptance, and resignation. Leaders reported different strategies for dealing with their individual circumstances. While some resorted to independent problem solving, others such as Mary (case 13) chose to get the "whole system in the room," by which she meant taking into consideration the voices of all the parties involved, rather than resorting to problem solving on her own or with individual parties.

Uncertainty Reduction Theory (URT)

Developed by Berger & Calabrese (1975), URT is a communications theory in the post-positivist tradition. They posit that in initial interactions, people strive to reduce uncertainty, based on plausible outcomes. Knobloch (2008) writes: "URT identifies two types of uncertainty that arise in dyadic interaction: 'Cognitive uncertainty' refers to the doubts people experience about their own beliefs and the beliefs of others. 'Behavioral uncertainty' refers to the questions people have about their own actions and the actions of others" (Knobloch, 2008, p. 134). The theory makes an important distinction between uncertainty and ambiguity. The latter is an objective state triggered in part by insufficient or conflicting information; however, the former is a subjective condition that occurs when we become aware of ambiguity. Several axioms are also proposed to emphasize the positive or negative relationship between uncertainty and communication.

As an example, our uncertainty may be high when we meet a total stranger at the mall and engage in a superficial conversation. As we begin to share with each other, information such as our occupations, likes, and dislikes while exploring similar interests, the uncertainty reduces and a sense of closeness and intimacy starts to develop between us.

Janice (case 10) a leader in academia shared in the interview that she tends to feel very uncomfortable if she does not know the reason behind a coworker's silence. She commented that she liked to feel needed, and not knowing why someone was quiet, put her in a state of ambiguity and frustration. To deal with that state, she sought out more information from the person. If however, the person chose to not share, her ambiguity turned to uncertainty. She made an analogy with throwing random darts at a board, hoping that one would hit the bull's eye. She further added that she did not deal well with chaos, and constantly looked for certainty. Several leaders commented that the ambiguity they faced in the workplace was a source of great tension to them. The "Uncertainty Reduction Theory" (URT) helps explain the leaders' emotional reactions, which possibly emanated from their subjective state of mind.

Findings

The analysis indicates three important findings: a) The context in which leaders are embedded may not have a significant bearing on how they experience and make sense of negative capability, b) the majority of leaders interviewed appear to have a diminished capacity to contain uncertainty when faced with paradoxical dilemmas, and c) they resort to behaviors such as problem solving, consulting others, shutting down, and dispersing as a defense against the uncertainty.

Experiences and continuing research

In addition to the findings, I would like to share other experiences. As I undertook the study, I had speculated that negative capability was an ephemeral state of mind that may easily give way to an overwhelming need for certitude. I had also hoped, however, that there would be some leaders that could potentially stay in a reflective mindset while resisting the temptation to engage in dispersal. Clearly, that has not been the outcome of the study in all three contexts, namely academia, private practice, and business organizations. It seemed as though leaders tried to make sense of the phenomenon as it related to their emotional and psychological conditions such as uncertainty, doubt,

120

ambiguity, and perplexity, but found it difficult to relate those conditions to negative capability as a frame of mind.

Our internal conditions and the external environment are an inextricable reality that is difficult to disentangle or separate from. We can think of them as the life worlds in which we are immersed. When researching a phenomenon sideways, as I did, it was important to understand how the life worlds of participants helped shape their perception. In a recent conversation with two practicing phenomenologists, I wanted to understand from their perspective how one might make sense of a disposition such as negative capability. They referred me to the work of Schutz, who enriched phenomenology by adding a "sociological" dimension to the field.

Schutz (1970) writes about the "world of daily life" which he considers to be an intersubjective reality that existed long before we were born. It was interpreted by others, including our predecessors and is now available to us to make sense of, not only through our direct experiences, but also the experiences handed down to us by parents and teachers. We cannot extricate ourselves from those experiences and all reality is subject to, and made sense of through those paradigmatic lenses, worldviews, and frames.

I did not see any noticeable difference across the three contexts, as it pertained to the way leaders made sense of the phenomenon, which led me to believe that the workplace setting in which a leader is embedded may have little impact on how that individual deals with uncertainty. Perhaps a more telling indicator may be a leader's interpersonal style, such as "introversion" or "extroversion." Certain leaders volunteered this information without being asked for it. I suggest that introverts may have a greater propensity to hold the negative space than extroverts. This finding is not based on the study, but my own experience with negative capability over the last 10 years. My reasoning is that an introvert is already quite adept at containing inner impulses and feelings without the need for external validation or acting out. By contrast, extroverts need the external validation, which may put them at a disadvantage. It is a complex area that needs more research.

In future studies of a phenomenological nature, especially those that involve researching an abstract phenomenon such as negative capability, it may be helpful to invest more time into recruiting a purposive sample. It is not sufficient to take participants' assurances for granted that they comprehend the research topic. They must also demonstrate their understanding of it. Perhaps, they should be required to answer a short questionnaire or respond to a case scenario before they are finally selected.

I would also recommend that there be conformity between what is stated in the research question and what actually appears in the interview schedule. It is not advisable to assume that the participants will of their own volition reflect on the phenomenon if the researcher does not directly broach the topic. Novice researchers are ill advised to research a phenomenon sideways, notwithstanding the richness of data that such a study might eventually yield.

If this were a study involving the directly accessible and relatable experiences of participants, such as those who were involved in a natural disaster like a hurricane, the experience of first-generation Americans immigrating to the US from a completely alien culture, or even a study involving gay individuals, the data yielded would be different in nature. It would have been easier for participants to talk about their direct experiences because there is a commonality that is shared by them around a particular phenomenon. By adding an extra layer, we also end up compounding the complexity that must be worked through before a meaningful study can be conducted. The multidisciplinary focus of this study was challenging, but I took the risk to enter uncharted territory. As I conclude this dissertation, I am not aware of any studies that have already been published at the doctoral level on negative capability. I may be pioneering research in this area.

As I have previously stated, my recommendation for those who want to use the IPA methodology effectively, would be to engage a corpus that does not exceed 6 participants. A smaller corpus enables a researcher to conduct a through microanalysis and interpret data at the descriptive, linguistic, and conceptual levels. It is easier to identify convergences, divergences, and contradictions when the accounts of a smaller number of participants are being analyzed.

Deviant finding: Obsessive Compulsive Disorder (OCD) and Negative Capability

In case 1 with Amanda, there was a unique connection established between negative capability and obsessive-compulsive disorder (OCD). While this was not a shared theme among leaders, I consider it to be worthy of further exploration. In IPA studies, it is not completely unusual to discover something that at first seems to have no relevance to the study phenomenon, and yet, adds something of great value to the project. I share this finding here with the hope that it may contribute something of value to the existing body of qualitative literature on OCD.

"OCD is one of the most common causes of disability worldwide" (Phillipson, 2014). The author classifies OCD in 3 broad categories:

1. "Classical OCD," which involves the performance of rituals to reduce anxiety.

2. "Over-responsibility and guilt OCD" in which sufferers think that they are responsible for the welfare of others close to them and feel accountable if they are not able to do it successfully or feel unworthy of it.

3. "Obsessional thinking OCD" which does not involve rituals, but sufferers experience intrusive, alarming, and persistent thoughts that come from nowhere.

In order to better understand the correlation of negative capability and OCD, I paraphrase Keats' definition. "Negative Capability is the capacity to remain in mysteries, doubts, and uncertainty without the irritable reaching after fact and reason." Remaining in mysteries, doubts, and uncertainty for any length of time is not easy. OCD is a chronic "doubting condition," one in which the sufferer is overwhelmed by recurring and intrusive thoughts. As Amanda (case 1) shared: "There is absolute terror in that space. There will be explosive behavior if you get between the thought and the ritual." As the patient's anxiety is heightened, so is the impulse to alleviate it by performing a ritual. While performing the ritual is a patient's defense mechanism for managing and containing the anxiety, it serves to both alleviate and perpetuate it. The key would be to help the patient break the link between a thought and a ritual. Not performing a ritual would be tantamount to resisting the impulse to reach out with action, fact, and reason. It is hoped that this initiative may help alleviate the suffering of those who are afflicted with moderate to severe OCD.

Redefining negative capability: Postmodern consideration and implications

This study is important because an increasing number of professions demand that leaders be able to deploy negative capability as part of their jobs. The construct is fascinating, but when it comes to practice, people seem to find it challenging. There may be a need to develop a postmodern definition of negative capability that is more pragmatic and realistic for our times. As consultants and educators, we are called upon to become double agents (Voller, 2014). On one hand we are viewed as experts that give clients advice; however, on the other, it is our ignorance and capacity to remain open to discomfort, uncertainty and ambiguity that may produce any significant changes. Even the most experienced professionals agree that staying in the negative space (at the edge of knowing and not knowing) can be quite painful. They think of it in terms of mindful awareness which may be defined as "a state of psychological freedom that occurs when attention remains quiet and limber, without attachment to any particular point of view" (Martin, 1997, pp. 291-312). Perhaps, the difficulty people have in understanding the expression is that it appears to be an oxymoron; the words negative and capability seem to be antithetical and cancel each other out. We are not conditioned to think of the word "negative" as having any positive connotation and attribute only positive meanings to the word "capability."

The practice of negative capability presents a strange paradox, as we attempt to hold two contrasting and conflicting attitudes together, resulting in a state of tension. What makes the predicament even harder is that the two positions (polarities) may not necessary present us with an easy choice (either-or). They very often are complementary and interdependent, not mutually exclusive. And yet, the creative tension that we speak of is a result of contradiction, which is necessary for discourse and dialogue. While homogeneity and consensus are congenial, contradiction and difference, on the other hand can be terrifying.

Research scholars, especially those that are engaged in qualitative studies, may find that the practice of negative capability may provide a means of holding their anxieties and tensions in what can be a very messy process that is replete with uncertainty. Denzin and Lincoln (1994) write, "The field of qualitative research is defined by a series of tensions, contradictions, and hesitations" (Denzin & Lincoln, 1994, p. 15).

There is not a definitive stance on what constitutes good qualitative research. On the one hand, a researcher with a post-positivist mindset who takes a detached, hands-off approach in the interview may create more objective space; however, on the other, the individual may also be viewed as disinterested and distant. So how does one hold this difficult dialectic?

Glesne and Peshkin (1992) suggest that a successful researcher is one who can remain "paradoxically bilateral" (dominant, but also submissive). Oakley (1981), a feminist researcher contends that the goal in most interviews is best achieved when the interviewers and interviewees are in a nonhierarchical relationship, with the former willing to invest their personal identities in the relationship. I made an attempt in this study to remain paradoxically bilateral---subjective and objective at the same time. The study was full of challenges and contradiction, and yet, it was in the very nature of the inquiry that I discovered new insights. I would not have been able to engage in the study if I could not practice negative capability. Scholars with a positivist mindset, entering qualitative research for the first time, may do well to cultivate a negative capability frame of mind. IPA study 1 featured in chapter 3 is interesting from this standpoint.

Being in a negative capability mindset is like undertaking a journey without a clear destination. Phenomenologists are called upon to constantly work in liminal spaces. Bentz & Rehorick (2008) using the metaphor of a wild horse to describe the final stage in hermeneutic phenomenology write: "In level 3, one rides the wild horse, taking the risk of ending up in a place one did not expect. One lets the horse become the guide" (Bentz & Rehorick, 2008, p. 21). It may be that in postmodern times, we need to think of negative capability as a "state of questioning," and allow ourselves to be guided by inquiry, while resisting the temptation to understand why we are in that space in the first place. In attempting to understand something by reaching for the doctrinaire of knowledge, we are taking flight to the world of certitude that is ephemeral at best. We are once again thrust into paradoxical dilemmas that are unavoidable.

It may be that in contemporary times, staying in the present without regressing to the past or fleeing into the future is all that we can learn to do. Attending experiential conferences in the Tavistock tradition is a unique way to cultivate a "here-and-now" awareness that has the capacity to contain perplexing experiences. It provides an opportunity for members to join a temporary institution for a few days or even a of weeks and experience what it is like to face and make sense of anxiety. Such experiences bring us face-to-face with the unconscious and out of awareness processes that we do not think of in the normal course.

I realize that defining negative capability is attempting to do the impossible. Keats only used the expression once in a letter to his brothers in 1817 as he talks about his role model, Shakespeare. I paraphrase: "It is when man is capable of being in mysteries, doubts, and uncertainty without the irritable reaching after fact and reason." In phenomenological studies one is not educating a reader about what is being researched, but simply leaving open the possibility that the reader may immerse in your life world and make sense of the phenomenon. For me, the lure and seduction of negative capability is in its ephemeral, fleeting, and mercurial qualities. It keeps one guessing and even wanting more.

Nearly 200 years after its coinage by a romantic poet in his early twenties, negative capability continues to be raised by scholars to a canonical status. There is no finality, and so, if I were to put such a definition around something so elusive, I am indulging in the pursuit of knowledge, as opposed to staying with the not knowing. If I profess to know all that there is to know about negative capability, I will have failed miserably in this endeavor. What I hope I have tried to do is engage the reader's questioning mind. Batchelor (1990) suggests that where there is great questioning, there is great awakening. Where there is little questioning, there is little awakening. Where there is no questioning, there is no awakening.

One of the goals of a phenomenological study of this nature, especially one that deals with such an aesthetic phenomenon, is to invoke a reader's "poetic sensibilities." van Manen (1990, p. 13) suggests that phenomenology is not unlike poetry. "It is a poetizing project; it tries an incantative, evocative speaking, a primal telling, wherein we aim to involve the voice in an original singing of the world." More recently, he suggests: "Not unlike the poet, the phenomenologist directs the gaze towards the regions where meaning originates, wells up, percolates through the porous membranes of past sedimentations and then infuses us, permeates us, infects us, touches us, stirs us, exercises a formative effect" (van Manen, 2007, p. 12).

126

Understanding that the void of "not knowing" is the womb for new creations and breakthroughs, is perhaps a powerful enough awareness that may lead to change and transformation in society. It is my hope that many courageous leaders will continue on that journey and set an example for others who are too anxious or fearful to embark on that path.

Appendix A

References

Afifi, W.A., & Matsunaga, M. (2008). Three approaches to a multifarious process. In *Engaging Theories in Interpersonal Communication.* L. Baxter & D. Braithewaite (Eds.). London: Sage

Altman, I., Vinsel, A., & Brown, B. (1981). Dialectic conceptions in social psychology: An application to social penetration and privacy regulation. In L. Berkowitz (Ed). *Advances in Experimental Social Psychology* (Vol. 14, pp. 107-160). NY: Academic Press

Argyris, C. (1990). *Overcoming organizational defenses.* NJ: Prentice Hall

Argyris, C., & Schon, D. (1978). *Organizational learning: A theory of action perspective* Reading, MA: Addison-Wesley

Babrow, A.S. (1992). Communication and problematic integration: Understanding diverging probability and value, ambiguity, ambivalence, and impossibility. *Communication Theory, 2,* 95-130

Bakhtin, M.M. (1981). *The dialogic imagination.* Austin: University of Texas Press

Bakhtin, M.M. (1984). *Problems of Dostoevsky's poetics* (C. Emerson, Ed. and Trans.). Minneapolis: University of Minnesota Press

Bakhtin, M.M. (1986). *Speech genres and other late essays.* (C. Emerson & M. Holquist, Eds. V. McGee, Trans.). Austin; University of Texas Press

Batchelor, S. (1990). *The faith to doubt: Glimpses of Buddhist uncertainty.* Berkeley, CA: Parallax Press

Batchelor, S. (2000). *Verses from the center: A Buddhist vision of the sublime.* New York: Riverhead Books

Batchelor, S. (2000). *Negative Capability, Emptiness, Nagarjuna, and Keats.* Podcast of lecture delivered at the Trinity College, CT on April 11, 2000. URL: http://www.radio4all.net/index.php/program/1817 (accessed on July 17, 2013)

Bate, W.J. (1963). *Negative capability.* In Keats (1964): A Collection of Critical Essays, Ed. Walter Jackson Bate pp. 51-68

Bate, W.J. (1964). *Keats: A collection of critical essays.* (Ed. W.J. Bate). NJ: Prentice-Hall, Inc.

Bate, W.J. (2012). *Negative Capability: The intuitive approach in Keats.* Contra Mundum Press

Bateson, G. (1972a). Double bind, 1969. In G. Bateson, *Steps to an ecology of mind* (pp. 271-278). San Francisco: Chandler

Bateson, G. (1974). *Mind and nature: A necessary unity.* NY: Dutton

Baxter, L.A. (2006). Communication as dialogue. In G.J. Shepherd, J. St. John & T. Striphas (Eds.). *Communication as Perspectives on Theory.* (pp. 101-109). CA: Sage

Baxter, L.A., & Montgomery, B.M. (1996). *Relating: Dialogues and dialectics.* NY: Guilford Press

Baxter, L.A. & Braithwaite, D.O. (Eds). (2008). *Engaging theories in interpersonal communication.* LA: Sage

Bentz, V.M., & Rehorick, D.A. (2008). *Transformative phenomenology.* New York: Lexington Books

Berger, C.R., & Calabrese, R.J. (1975). Some explorations in initial interaction and beyond: Toward a developmental theory of interpersonal communication. *Human Communication Research, 1,* 99-112

Bion, W.R. (1961). *Experiences in groups.* London: Tavistock Publications

Bion, W.R. (1967). Notes on memory and desire. *Psychoanalytic Forum, 2:* 271-80

Bion, W.R. (1970). *Attention and interpretation.* London: Tavistock Publications

Bion, W.R. (1984a). *Attention and interpretation.* London: Karnac

Bollas, C. (1987). *The shadow of the object: Psychoanalysis of the unthought known.* New York: Columbia University Press

Bolman, L.G., & Deal, T.E. (2008). *Reframing organization: Artistry, choice, and leadership.* CA: Jossey-Bass

Brashers, D.E. (2001a). Communication and uncertainty management. *Journal of Communication, 51,* 477-497.

Bush, D. (1937). *John Keats: His life and writings.* London: Macmillan

Chow, R. (2012). *Entanglements, or transmedial thinking about capture*. NC: Duke University Press

Cooper, R., Fleischer, A., & Cotton, F.A. (2012). Building connections: An Interpretative Phenomenological Analysis of qualitative research students' learning experiences. *The Qualitative Report*. Vol. 17, T&L Article 1, 1-16

Cranton, P. (1994). *Understanding and promoting transformative learning: A guide for educators of adults*. San Francisco: Jossey-Bass

Cusa, N. (1440). *Learned ignorance* (publisher unknown)

Czander, W.M. (1993). *The psychodynamics of work and organization*. New York; The Guilford Press

Denzin, N.K. & Lincoln, U.S. (Eds.). (1994). *Handbook of qualitative research*. CA: Sage

Dewey, J. (1929a). *The quest for certainty: A study of the relation of knowledge and action*. New York: Minton, Balch.

Dilthey, W. (1979). *Wilhelm Dilthey: Pioneer of the human studies*. (Trans. H.P. Rickman). London: University of California Press

Eigen, M. (1998). *The psychoanalytic mystique*. London: Free Association Books

Elson, L.G. (2010). *Paradox lost: A cross-contextual definition of levels of abstraction*. NJ: Hampton Press, Inc.

Fitzgerald, C., & Howe-Walsh, L. (2008). Self-initiated expatriates: An Interpretative Phenomenological Analysis of professional female expatriates, in *International Journal of Business and Management*. Vol 3, No. 10

Foucault, M. (1972). *The archaeology of knowledge*. London: Tavistock

Fraher, A.L. (2004). *A history of group study and psychodynamic organizations*. London: Free Association Books

Fraher, A.L. (2004). Systems psychodynamics: The formative years of an interdisciplinary field at the Tavistock Institute. *History of Psychology*. 7(1), 65-84

French, R. (1999). The importance of capacities in psychoanalysis and the language of human development. *International Journal of Psychoanalysis,* 80(6): 1215-1226

French, R. (2000). Negative capability, dispersal and the containment of emotion. *Bristol Business School Teaching and Research Review*, Issue 3, Summer 2000, ISSN 1468-4578

French, R., & Simpson, P. (2000). *Learning at the edges between knowing and not knowing*: Translating Bion. Organizational and Social Dynamics Journal, 1(1), 54-77

French, R., Simpson, P., & Harvey, C. (2001). *Negative capability: The key to creative leadership.* Paper presented at the ISPSO symposium, Paris, France

Gadamer, Hans-Georg. (1990). *Truth and method.* New York: Crossroad

Giddens, A. (1987). *Social theory and modern sociology.* CA: Stanford University Press

Glesne, C. & Peshkin, A. (1992). *Becoming qualitative researchers: An introduction.* NY: Longman

Goffman, E. (1963). *Stigma: Notes on the management of spoiled identity.* NY: Simon & Schuster

Goffman, E. (1974). *Frame analysis.* NY: Harper & Row

Greenleaf, R.K. (2008). *The servant as leader.* IN: The Greenleaf Center for Servant Leadership

Greenwood, D., & Levin, M. (1998). *Introduction to action research.* London: Sage

Hammersley, M., & Atkinson, P. (1990). *Ethnography: Principles in practice.* London: Routledge

Hazlitt, W. (1805). *An essay on the principles of human action: Being an argument in favor of the natural disinterestedness of the human mind.* London: J. Johnson

Hefferon, K., & Gil-Rodriguez, E. (2011). Interpretative Phenomenological Analysis. *The Psychologist,* Vol. 24, Part 10

Hegel, G.W.F. (1977). *Phenomenology of spirit.* New York: Oxford University Press

Hegel, G.W.F. (2003). *The phenomenology of mind.* New York: Dover

Heidegger, M. (1962). *Being and time.* Oxford: Blackwell

Heidegger, M. (1971). *Poetry, language, thought.* NY: Fitzhenry & Whiteside Ltd.

Heidegger, M. (1977). *Basic writings.* NY: Harper & Row Publishers

Heidegger, M. (1999). *Ontology: The hermeneutics of facticity.* (Trans. John van Buren). Indianapolis, IN: Indiana University Press

Husserl, E. (1970). *The crisis of European sciences and transcendental phenomenology.* (Trans. David Carr). Evanston: Northwestern University Press

Israelstam, K.V. (2007). Creativity and dialectical phenomena: From dialectical edge to dialectical space. *International Journal of Psychoanalysis,* 88, pp. 59-607

Jerpbak, M.R. (2006). *Being like my father: A phenomenological study of fathers' lived experiences* (doctoral dissertation). Minneapolis, MN: University of Minnesota

Jacques, E. (1955). Social systems as a defence against persecutory and depressive anxiety, in M.Klein, P. Heimann, and R.E. Money-Kyrle (Eds.), *New Directions in Psychoanalysis.* London; Tavistock

Johnson, B. (1992). *Polarity management: Identifying and managing unsolvable problems.* MA: HRD Press

Keats, J. (1817). *The Letters of John Keats, 1814-1821.* 2 Vols. Ed. Hyder Edward Rollins. Cambridge, MA: Harvard University Press

Kegan, R. (1994). *In over our heads: The mental demands of modern life.* MA: Harvard University Press

Knobloch, L.K. (2008). Communicating under conditions of ambiguity. In *Engaging Theories in Interpersonal Communication.* L. Baxter & D. Braithwaite (Eds.). London; Sage

Kolb, D. (1984). *Experiential learning: Experience as the source of learning and development.* NJ: Prentice Hall

Korzybski, A. (1933). *Science and sanity.* NY: International Non-Aristotelian Library

Laiken, M.E. (2001). *Models of organizational learning: Paradoxes and best practices in the postindustrial workplace.* In conference proceedings of the 21st OD World Congress, Vienna, Austria: July 16-21, 2001. Charles A. Rarick (Ed.) pp. 1-16

Laiken, M.E. (2002). *Managing the action/reflection polarity through dialogue: A path to transformative learning.* NALL Working Paper #53 (2002): Toronto, Canada

Lao, Tzu. (2006). *Tao ching.* Trans. John C.H. Wu. Boston: Shambhala

Lewin, K. (1951). *Field theory in social science.* NY: Harper & Row

Martin, J. (1997). Mindfulness: A proposed common factor. *Journal of Psychotherapy Integration.* Vol. 7 Number 4 291-312

Martin, M. (2000). *The uses of understanding in social science: Verstehen.* NJ: Transaction Publishers

Menzies, I.E.P. (1960). A case study in the functioning of social systems as a defense against anxiety. *Human Relations,* 13: 95-121

Mezirow, J. (1991). *Transformative dimensions of adult learning.* UK: Brookfield Publishing

Mezirow, J. & Associates. (2000). *Learning as transformation: Critical perspectives on a theory in progress.* CA: Jossey-Bass

Merleau-Ponty, M. (1962). *Phenomenology of perception.* (Trans. Colin Smith). London: Routledge

Merleau-Ponty, M. (1974). *Phenomenology, language and sociology.* London: Heinemann Educational Books Ltd.

Meyer, J.H.F & Land, R. (2006). Implications of threshold concepts for course design and evaluation, in Meyer, J.H.F., & Land, R. (eds.). *Overcoming barriers to student understanding: Threshold concepts and troublesome knowledge.* London and New York: Routledge

Molino, A. (Ed). (1998). *The couch and the tree: Dialogues in psychoanalysis and Buddhism.* New York: North Point Press

Morgan, G. (1986). *Images of organization.* CA: Sage

Needleman, J. (1990). *Lost Christianity: A journey of rediscovery to the centre of Christian experience.* Shaftesbury, Dorset: Element Books

Nitsun, M. (1996). *The anti-group: Destructive forces in the group and their creative potential.* London: Routledge

Oakley, A. (1981). Interviewing women: A contradiction in terms. In *Doing Feminist Research,* Ed. H. Roberts, pp. 30-61

Ogden, T.H. (1929a). The dialectically constituted /decentered subject of psychoanalysis. *International Journal of Psychoanalysis,* 73: 517-26

Phillipson, S. (2014). *Obsessional thinking.* In Anxiety Care UK. http://www.anxietycare.org.uk/docs/obsessionalthinkingonline.asp Retrieved on February 26, 14

Prus, R. (1996). *Symbolic interaction and ethnographic research: Intersubjectivity and the study of human lived experience.* NY: State University of New York Press

Raab, N. (1997). Becoming an expert in knowing: Reframing teacher as consultant. *Management Learning.* Vol. 28(2): 161-175. London: Sage

Reason, P. (1994). Three approaches to participative inquiry. In N.K. Denzin and Y.S. Linclon, *Handbook of Qualitative Research.* Thousand Oaks, CA: Sage

Ricoeur, P. (1970). *Freud and philosophy: An essay on interpretation.* New Haven: Yale University Press

Roca, J. (2009). *Assessing leaders' negative capability: The negative capability 360 feedback tool.* Press release accessed on February 21, 2014 from http://www.prlog.org/10350936-assessing-leaders-negative-capability-the-negative-capability-360-feedback-tool.html

Rollins, E. (1958). *Letters of John Keats* (Vol 1, p. 191). MA: Harvard University Press

Rose, K., & Webb, C. (1998). Analyzing data: Maintaining rigor. In *Qualitative Health Research,* ISSN: 1049-7323; Vol. 8 No. 4; p. 556

Sartre, J.P. (1948). *Existentialism and humanism.* (P. Mairet, Trans.). London: Methuen

Schein, E.H. (1999). *Process consultation revisited.* MA: Addison-Wesley

Schleiermacher, F. (1998). *Hermeneutics and criticism and other writings* (A, Bowie, Trans.). Cambridge: CUP

Schutz, A. (1970). *On phenomenology and social relations.* Chicago: The University of Chicago Press

Scott, N.A., Jr. (1969). *Negative capability: Studies in the new literature and the religious situation.* CT: Yale

Simpson, P., & French, R. (2006). Negative capability and the capacity to think in the present moment: Some implications for leadership practice. *Leadership*: 2; 245 DOI: 10.1177/1742715006062937

Smith, J.A. (2007). Hermeneutics, human science, and health: Linking theory and practice. *International Journal of Qualitative Studies in Health and Well-Being,* 2, 3-11

Smith, J.A., Flowers, P., & Larkin, M. (2009). *Interpretative phenomenological analysis: Theory, method and research.* London: Sage

Star, S.L. (2007). Living grounded theory: Cognitive and emotional forces of pragmatism. *Sage Handbook of Grounded Theory*. Eds. Antony Bryant & Kathy Charmaz. LA: Sage

Steir, E. (1991). *Reflexivity and methodology : An ecological constructionism*. In E Steir (Ed.). London : Sage

Suler, J.R. (1993). *Contemporary psychoanalysis and eastern thought*. NY: State University of New York Press

Suzuki, D.T. (1972). *The Zen doctrine of no-mind: The significance of the Sutra of Hui-Neng*. York Beach, ME: Samuel Weiser

Turner, V. (1969). *The ritual process: Structure and anti-structure*. Chicago: Aldine Publishing

Turner, V. (1974). *Dramas, fields, and metaphors: Symbolic action in human society*. Ithaca, NY: Cornell University Press

Turner V. (1994). *Betwixt and between: The liminal period in rites of passage*. In Betwixt and Between: Patterns of Masculine and Feminine Initiation, Eds. Louise Carus Mahdi, Steven Foster & Meredith Little

Van Gennep A. (1960). *The rites of passage*. London: Routledge

Van Manen, M. (1990). *Researching lived experience: Human science for an action sensitive pedagogy*. Ontario, Canada: State University of New York Press

Van Manen, M. (2007). Phenomenology of practice. *Phenomenology & Practice, 1*(1), 11

Voller, D. (2014). Negative Capability. *Contemporary Psychotherapy*. *http://contemporarypsychotherapy.org/vol-2-no-2/negative-capability/* Retrieved on February 26, 2014

Voloshinov, V.N. (1973). *Marxism and the philosophy of language* (L. Matejka & I.R. Titunik, Trans.). MA: Harvard University Press

Ward, A. (1963). *John Keats: The making of a poet*. London: Secker and Warburg

Webb, C.W. (1992). The use of first person in academic writing: Objectivity, language, and   gatekeeping. *Journal of Advanced Nursing, 17*, 747-752

Weick, K. (1979). *The social psychology of organizing*. MA: Addison-Wesley

Wilden, A. (1972). *System and structure: Essays in communication and exchange.*
    London: Tavistock

Winnicott, D.W. (1965). *The maturational process and the facilitating environment:*
    Studies in the theory of emotional development. London: Hogarth

Winnicott, D.W. (1986). *Holding and interpretation: Fragment of an analysis.* New York:
    Grove Press

Yardley, L. (2000). Dilemmas in qualitative health research. *Psychology & Health, 15,*
    215-22

Endnotes

1   Also used here from the standpoint of Bion's notion of attention and the Buddhist doctrine of mindfulness, both of which call for an isolation from preoccupying mental processes in order to learn from experience

2   See Fraher, A.L. (2004). *Systems Psychodynamics: The formative years of an interdisciplinary field at the Tavistock Institute.* History of Psychology. 7(1), 65-84. Fraher's (2004) study of the history of psychodynamic organizations also provides an in-depth exploration of many psychodynamic constructs now used in the field of group dynamics.

3   See Fraher, A.L. (2004). *A history of group study and psychodynamic organizations.* London: Free Association Books

4   Similar to Nagarjuna's doctrine of "sunyata" (emptiness). Nagarjuna is also credited with the dialectic and development of the "two-truths doctrine," i.e. "paramartha sathya" (ultimate reality) and "samvrti sathya" (superficial reality)

5   Japanese Buddhist term for "standing at the crossroads"

6   Japanese Buddhist term for "awakening" or "enlightenment"

7   Used in Zen teachings to provoke doubt and uncertainty in the student

8   See Bateson (1969); Elson (2010) for a detailed explication of "double-bind" theory

9   The work of Hegel and Marx, also ancient Indian (Jainism) dialectics and philosophy of pluralistic thinking is key. See the Jain doctrine of "Anekantavada" (non-exclusivity and multiplicity of viewpoints). The ancient parable of the "Blind Men and an Elephant" nicely illustrates the doctrine.

Appendix B

Demographic Information Gathering Form

Name: _____Age_____

Phone: _____ Address: _____

City/ST/Zip _____ Email address:

_____

Preferred method of contact: _____ phone _____ email

Where do you work: _____

Ethnicity/Race (choose as many as apply):

_____ American Indian _____ Caucasian _____ Asian _____ Black _____ Hispanic

_____ Number of years doing work: _____

Appendix C

Preliminary Email Inquiry

Dear Colleague:

I'd like to introduce myself and ask for your assistance with my doctoral study. The study is conducted as part of my doctoral dissertation and is entitled "Negative Capability: A Phenomenological Study of Lived Experience at the Edge of Certitude and Incertitude."

I have been working in the field of organizational development, including training and consulting for over 12 years and supporting those who work in many diverse fields. In my work with these individuals, I have become very aware of the complexity of their jobs and what their roles entail. I have come to appreciate and acknowledge the challenges of their positions and what it takes to hold them.

As a doctoral student at Fielding Graduate Institute, I have been exploring the competency of "negative capability." Coined by the English romantic poet John Keats, it is a unique capacity to stay in mysteries, doubts, uncertainty, and ambiguity without irritably reaching after fact and reason. As part of my graduate work and the subject of my dissertation, I am conducting research into this unique competency. I am speculating that negative capability may be a very transient stage in what may develop into something more ongoing. It can be defined as a state of mind where the individual is trying to hold together what appear to be contradictory or opposing values. Tensions of this nature may arise when the workplace is going through significant change and uncertainty, during interpersonal conflict with peers, clients, and direct reports, and other situations where leaders are called upon to exercise great restraint when the pressure to react may be strong. Some examples of this tension may be autonomy vs. connectedness; favoritism vs. impartiality; and spontaneity vs. predictability. More information can be provided upon request.

My study has been designed to learn from the experiences of those who are called upon to practice this skill as part of their work and/or who work in situations that require them to deploy this skill.

And this is where I am asking for your assistance. I am seeking to interview key participant leaders from academia, private practice (self-employed OD consultants, coaches, management consultants etc.), and business organizations in order to learn about their experiences with uncertainty and conflict in the workplace. The selection criteria are outlined below:

1. Participants must be between the ages of 35-65 and currently employed or self-employed (if in private practice).

2. Participants must be US citizens or permanent residents.

3. Participants must have a minimum of 5 years work experience.

4. Participants must have experienced or currently experiencing uncertainty and conflict in the workplace (see examples in paragraph 3 above)

5. Participants should be willing to actively participate and share their narratives with the investigator in a private interview lasting 90 minutes (with an extra 10 minutes for set up). If meeting face-to-face is not feasible, the interview may be conducted via Skype, Go To Meeting, or telephone. Interview proceedings will be digitally recorded.

If you meet the selection criteria and are interested in participating in this pilot, or if you know of others who might be interested in participating, I would very much appreciate your sharing their contact information with me or having you forward this email to them for their consideration. Anyone who is referred or who contacts me about participating will have their participation kept strictly confidential – so I will not be able to let you know if any people you may refer have agreed to participate.

Thank you for your time and consideration. I may be reached at 610-517-5381 if you have questions or please respond to this email and I will be happy to address your questions and concerns. My email address is abehal@email.fielding.edu

Sincerely,

Anil Behal

Appendix D

Participant Recruitment Letter

Dear:

_____ has suggested that I contact you about some work that I am doing.

I have been working in the field of organizational development for many years. In my work with professionals, I have become very aware of the roles that they hold and what it takes to discharge their roles. I have come to appreciate and acknowledge the challenges and professional dedication of leaders who practice "negative capability" as part of their jobs. I define negative capability below.

Coined by the English romantic poet John Keats, it is a unique capacity to stay in mysteries, doubts, uncertainty, and ambiguity without irritably reaching after fact and reason. As part of my graduate work at Fielding Graduate University, Santa Barbara, California, and the subject of my doctoral dissertation, I am conducting research into this unique competency. I am speculating that negative capability may be a very transient stage in what may develop into something more ongoing. It can be defined as a state of mind where the individual is trying to hold together what appear to be contradictory or opposing values. Tensions of this nature may arise when the workplace is going through significant change and uncertainty, during interpersonal conflict with peers, clients, and direct reports, and other situations where leaders are called upon to exercise great restraint when the pressure to react may be strong. Some examples of this tension may be autonomy vs. connectedness; favoritism vs. impartiality; and spontaneity vs. predictability. More information can be provided upon request.

Because of your years of experience as a leader, I am inviting you to participate in my doctoral study, which would take approximately 90 minutes of your time in a private interview with me. The study is conducted as part of my doctoral dissertation.

My study entitled "Negative Capability: A Phenomenological Study of Lived Experience at the Edge of Certitude and Incertitude" has been designed to learn more about leaders who work in situations that require them to regularly work in uncertain and ambiguous situations.

The interview will be focused on your past and current lived experiences of "negative capability" around specific episodes at work where you may have experienced significant ongoing anxiety or conflict. You have the right to not answer any question and to stop and leave the interview at any time. Your participation in any and all of the interviews is completely voluntary. If you choose not to participate or to withdraw from the study at any time, there is no penalty or consequences. Here are the selection criteria:

1. Participants must be between the ages of 35-65 and currently employed or self-employed (if in private practice).

2. Participants must be US citizens or permanent residents.

3. Participants must have a minimum of 5 years work experience.

4. Participants must have experienced or currently experiencing negative capability as a result of sustained uncertainty and conflict in the workplace (see examples in paragraph 3 above)

5. Participants should be willing to actively participate and share their narratives with the researcher in a private interview lasting 90 minutes (with an extra 10 minutes for set up). If meeting face-to-face is not feasible, the interview may be conducted via Skype, Go To Meeting, or telephone. Interview proceedings will be digitally recorded.

You may or may not experience any direct benefits from the interview process; however, your participation in the study may help provide a better understanding of the experiences of others who hold similar roles. Your interviews will be used to identify themes and patterns related to the data that we record, collect, and analyze.

The foreseeable risks or discomforts for you as a participant in this study are minimal. Should you experience any negative effects from the interview process, counseling or other support services may be identified. The security of data and interactions over the Internet cannot be guaranteed; therefore there may be a slight chance that the information you share or send will not be secure. The collection of these data is not expected to present any risk greater than what you might experience when sending and/or receiving information over the Internet.

If you agree to participate, you will be asked to consent to having your interviews digitally recorded so that a transcript can be created and used to better understand the themes and patterns that may emerge concerning your and others' experiences. The interview will not be taped without your permission. If you agree to the recording, you will be provided with a transcript of the interview upon request. If there are inaccuracies or things you wish to have removed from the transcript, you will have the opportunity to have those removed and not used in the study. After the interview is completed and recording archived, the transcript will be sent to you in the form of an electronic document and you will then be called to find out if anything is inaccurate or needs to be removed.

All of the information gathered in this study is confidential. In order to maintain confidentiality, you will be asked to choose a pseudonym that will be used throughout the study to conceal your identity. Audiotapes, transcriptions, consent forms, and all other study-related information will be kept in a secure location throughout the study. When the study is complete, information gathered during the study will be retained for no more than three years to assure that any questions that may arise related to the study can be tracked and then that information will be destroyed.

Only your chosen pseudonym will be used in any and all of these formats.

If you have any questions regarding the study, please contact me at 610-517-5381 or my committee chair, Dr. Robert Silverman (360-566-1080). If you have any questions about your rights as a participant in this research or if you feel you have been placed at risk, please contact the Institutional Review Board at Fielding Graduate University, irb@fielding.edu or (805) 690-4388

Two copies of the Consent Form to participate in this study are enclosed. If you choose to participate, please sign one copy and return it to me. The other copy is for your information and records.

Thank you for considering participation in my study.

Sincerely,

Anil Behal

This project is under the supervision of:
Fielding Graduate University

Robert Silverman, Ph.D.

2112 Santa Barbara Street

Santa Barbara, CA 93105 805-687-1099 Email address: rsilverman@fielding.edu

Fielding Graduate University

Informed Consent Form

Title of study:

Negative Capability: A Phenomenological Study of Lived Experience at the Edge of Certitude and Incertitude

You have been asked to participate in a study conducted by Anil Behal a doctoral student in the School of Human and Organizational Development at Fielding Graduate University, Santa Barbara, CA. This study is being supervised by Robert Silverman, Ph.D.

The research involves the study of "negative capability" and the experiences of leaders who use this skill. You are being asked to participate in this study because you meet the selection criteria.

The study involves individual interviews with participant leaders from academia, private practice, and business organizations. Each in-depth interview will last approximately 90 minutes, with an additional 10 minutes for set up. Interviews are preferably conducted face-to-face where possible or via Skype and/or Go To Meeting (web-based platform) or telephone, if meeting in person is not feasible. The interviews will be digitally recorded, and following the interview you may receive a copy of the digital file in the form of an electronic document. If you choose to delete information, the information will not be used in the study, and there will be no penalties. The information you provide will be kept strictly confidential. The informed consent forms and other identifying information will be kept separate from the data. (All materials will be kept in Anil's home office located at 725 George Drive, King of Prussia, Pennsylvania, in a locked file cabinet)

Digital recordings of the interviews will be listened to only by the Researcher and by Dr. Silverman, as study supervisor and Dissertation Chair. Any records that would identify you as a participant in this study, such as informed consent forms, will be destroyed by shredding and burning no later than 3 years after the study is completed.

You will be asked to provide a different name for any quotes that might be included in the study report. If any direct quotes will be used, permission will be sought from you first before including such material in the dissertation.

You may develop greater personal awareness of how your life experiences and your role as a professional have shaped career choices and you may have an even deeper appreciation of the work you do as a result of your participation in this research. The risks to you are considered minimal; there is a small chance that you may experience some emotional discomfort during or after your participation. The security of data transmitted over the Internet cannot be guaranteed; therefore there is a slight risk that information shared may not be secure. The collection of these data is not expected to present a risk greater than what you would encounter in everyday life when sending and/or receiving information over the Internet. Should you experience such discomfort, please contact Anil Behal for a list of counselors or therapists.

You may withdraw from this study at any time, either during or after your participation, without negative consequences. Should you withdraw, your data will be eliminated from the study and will be destroyed. No compensation will be provided for participation.

You may request a copy of the summary of the final results by indicating your interest at the end of this form. If you have any questions about any aspect of this study or your involvement, please tell the Researcher before signing this form. You may also contact the supervising faculty if you have questions or concerns about your participation in this study. The supervising faculty has provided contact information at the bottom of this form.

If you have questions or concerns about your rights as a research participant, contact the Fielding Graduate University Institutions Review Board office by email at irb@fielding.edu or by telephone at 805-898-4033.

If and when you agree to participate in this study, please sign the two copies of this informed consent form that have been provided and return one copy to Anil Behal at the address below. Signing the forms indicates that you have read, understood, and agree to participate in this research. Return one copy to the researcher and keep the other for your files. The Institutional Review Board of Fielding Graduate University retains the right to access the signed informed consent forms and other study documents.

NAME OF PARTICIPANT (please print) _____

SIGNATURE OF PARTICIPANT _____DATE

Supervisor: Robert Silverman, Ph.D.

Fielding Graduate University

2112 Santa Barbara Street, Santa Barbara, CA 93105

Researcher: Anil Behal

725 George Drive, King of Prussia, PA 19406

610-517-5381

Yes, please send a summary of the study results to:

_____

NAME (please print) _____Street Address_____

145

Appendix F

Telephone Script

Hi, this is Anil Behal a doctoral student at Fielding Graduate University. May I speak with_____?

First, I would like to thank you for participating in my doctoral study. The study is conducted as part of my doctoral dissertation.

As you know, we will be meeting for 90 minutes on_____ at _____ I wanted to confirm your availability on that day and also take about 10-15 minutes of your time today to briefly go over what we will be doing. Some of this information has already been sent to you via email, but I thought it would be helpful to reiterate it and answer any questions that you might have for me.

We will be meeting privately for 90 minutes during which I will be asking you specific questions pertaining to your past or present experiences with the study phenomenon. The interview is not meant to be an interrogation. It is a dialogue. As I wrote in my last email, your participation is completely voluntary; however, we do hope that you will be willing to openly share your experiences with me. You are also consenting to have these proceedings digitally recorded for the purpose of analysis. The security of data and interactions over the Internet cannot be guaranteed; therefore there may be a slight risk that the information you share or send will not be secure. The collection of these data is not expected to present any risk greater than what you might experience when sending and/or receiving information over the Internet.

Do you think that this might pose a problem for you? Great, I am happy to hear that you are okay with it!

As I previously wrote, the topic of my study is "Negative Capability: A Phenomenological Study of Lived Experience at the Edge of Certitude and Incertitude." Coined by the English romantic poet John Keats, it is a unique capacity to stay in mysteries, doubts, uncertainty, and ambiguity without irritably reaching after fact and reason. As part of my graduate work and the subject of my dissertation, I am conducting research into this unique competency. I am speculating that negative capability may be a very transient stage in what may develop into something more ongoing. It can be defined as a state of mind where the individual is trying to hold together what appear to be contradictory or opposing values. Tensions of this nature may arise when the workplace is going through significant change and uncertainty, during interpersonal conflict with peers, clients, and direct reports, and other situations where leaders are called upon to exercise great restraint when the pressure to react may be strong. Some examples of this tension may be autonomy vs. connectedness; favoritism vs. impartiality; and spontaneity vs. predictability. More information can be provided upon request. Thank you very much for your time and I look forward to meeting you on _____. You will also receive an email reminder on the morning of the meeting.

146

Interview schedule (dissertation study): Academia/Private Practice/Business (Individual

interviews): Duration: 90 minutes: Setup time: 10 minutes

1. How do you see yourself as a leader?
   Prompt: What is your preferred leadership style and philosophy? How do your peers and direct reports see you?

2. Can you tell me about a time when you found it hard to determine certain experiences?
   Prompt: What was it about these experiences that made it difficult to discuss or think about?

3. When confronted with a perplexing situation, how do you handle it?
   Prompt: What do you prefer doing; sitting with it patiently or resolving it promptly?

4. Think of an anxious time (episode) as a leader when you felt highly conflicted?
   Prompt: Tell me about this situation. What did it mean to you?

5. Looking back again, can you tell me more about this or another stressful situation?
   Prompt: Can you describe your state of mind as you think about these experiences?

6. What do you understand by paradoxical thinking in light of your specific experiences?
   Prompt: Can you give me an example of the paradoxical tension?

7. How do you negotiate and manage the tension at work?
   Prompt: Give me an example of how you might manage an ongoing situation such as an interdepartmental conflict.

8. It is said that great leaders deal well with ambiguity and conflict without seeking a quick resolution. Can you tell me about a time when you felt pressured to make a decision, but instead chose to sit and reflect on it before acting?

9. In your opinion, what might be the benefit of such a reflective state?

10. Summary and wrap up! Thanks for your time!

Box 1.1 (Initial list of themes)

Sense of identity

Sense of self

Framing

Reframing

Juxtaposition of personal and professional life

Obsessive Compulsive Disorder (OCD)

Ritualistic behavior

Levels of consciousness

Levels of abstraction

Holding polarities

Polarity management

Holding the tension of opposites

Negative Capability

Leadership and fellowship

Chaos, stress, emotion, danger, fear, terror

Servant leadership

Empowerment

Explosive behavior (consequence of getting between the thought and the ritual)

Repetition compulsion

Control as an illusion

Buddhism and uncertainty

Feelings of helplessness

Comfort with discomfort

Importance of not enabling the ritual

Dual lenses (observing ego, binocular vision)

Mud pit

Food metaphor (the thing that nourishes is also eliminated as waste)

Scotch: an acquired taste

Locked into experience of death

Cancer: you are suddenly part of a club you never wanted to join

Holding the paradox

Death of spouse and close friend

Kegan's work with levels of consciousness

One foot on the gas, the other one the breaks (goals and resistance)

Conflict also contains the resolution

Holding loss for the other

Managing polarities

Unfairly challenged, targeted at work

Social justice

Workplace bullying

Coping and defense mode

Managing and negotiating conflict

Being stripped of one's self

Survival instinct

Challenge

Liberating

Demeaning behavior

Triggering old memories/reliving past experiences

Emotionally shutting down

Values and tolerance

Being stripped of one's confidence

Core respect

Sense of validation

Compromise

Stamp out fires

Breaking down

Losing sleep

Emotions are a barometer

Interpersonal relationships

Dialectic of managing and negotiating tension

Black hole

Dependency needs

Micromanaging

Empowerment

Red flag goes up

Guards go up

Uncertainty

Yoga and meditation

Internal wine skin

Triangulation with boss and direct report

Unconscious collusion

Deadly embrace

Impasse

Career shift

Shingles

Mentoring

Making sense of difficult experiences

Cowboy riding into the sunset

Discomfort with silence

Scapegoating

Edge of knowing and not knowing

Corporate politics

Insomnia

Loss of control

Control is illusion

Diversity challenges, unconscious bias, minorities at work

Angry black male, fear of giving honest feedback, fear of discrimination

Betrayal at work

Paradoxical tension between serving students and serving employer

Experimenting

Action vs. reflection

Manipulation

Charismatic leader

Surrender of self and identity

Ex-marine

Boot camp

Death of spouse

Death of close friend

Gatekeeper for dying spouse

Not the brightest candle in church

Hospice

Dying

Problem solving

Panic mode

Transference and countertransference

Unthought known

Going against the grain

Contradiction and paradox

Complementarity and paradox

Jungian dialectic of opposites

Polarization

Between a rock and hard place

Giddy as a school-girl

Self-doubt, double guessing

Know yourself, choose yourself, grow yourself, give yourself to a higher cause

Handicaps

Emerging patterns

Diamond in the rough

Pygmalion effect

Self-preservation

Made in the USA
Monee, IL
22 June 2021

71889801R00094